REAL ESTATE INVESTING

Contents

Introduction

The potential to create passive income, dependable cash flow, tax advantages, diversification, and leverage are just a few advantages of real estate investing. Real estate investment trusts (REITs) allow you to diversify your holdings without actually owning, operating, or paying for the properties.

Our in-depth guide lays out exactly what is required to get the most gorgeous residences for a fair (or even below-market-value!) price. Despite covering a broad variety of assets, the focus of this book is on alternatives to commercial investments that are more comprehensible and acceptable to non-experts than commercial investments.

It is still possible to lose money while investing in reliable real estate even when long-term gains are anticipated. This is particularly true when making short-term real estate investments. It seems improbable that real estate prices would continue to increase annually. They don't, as many people in the late 2000s learned the hard way. Price reductions may be seen as minor setbacks on what should otherwise be an enjoyable trip when investing in real estate for the long term, as we suggest and do ourselves.

If you have the time and want to do so, we strongly recommend that you read this book from cover to cover. You may trade with confidence since it gives you a complete grasp of how to increase your profits while minimizing your risks in the real estate market. On the other hand, you can choose to focus on reading a few select topics. This book's writing style was among the aspects I like most.

Chapter One

Getting started with Real Estate

Are you certain that investing in real estate is the best move for you to make? Do you have a compelling motive for wanting to achieve your goals? Do you think you've mastered the ability to think like a profitable investor? Now that you're ready, start learning about real estate. When the student is ready, the teacher will arrive.

Real estate investing involves a substantial amount of data that is both frightening and difficult to comprehend. The goal of this section is to demystify the many complex facets of real estate investing and show you how to swiftly and simply comprehend such a challenging topic.

For instance, to find the fish in a vast river, trout fishermen split it into multiple little streams. The river flows swiftly and shallowly in some areas while being deep and slow in others. It may be intimidating and challenging to analyze a vast river, but by segmenting it into little streams, it becomes much easier to evaluate and identify the fish.

We'll follow the same method here and break down real estate investing into manageable parts, starting with the most fundamental, to help you better understand the many components. Real estate investing is about making money, which you may do now or in the future. As a consequence, real estate investing may be split into two groups: strategies for creating wealth and methods for getting quick cash.

Earning money today, sometimes referred to as quick cash, enables you to have money in your pocket right now. Many people right now are in desperate need of extra cash. Wealth accumulation, or the later creation of money, may bring in a steady stream of income or a sizeable sum of money over an extended period of time, all of which have their own benefits. Most significantly, investing in real estate is often tax-friendly. The Internal Revenue Service (IRS) has proposed a series of ideas that may make real estate cash-on-cash gains less tax-expensive.

It's crucial to ask oneself what they want to get out of real estate. If you already have a lot of liquid assets (cash), whether they come from a retirement account, an inheritance, a recently sold firm, or simply the constant accumulation of money in a bank account, put your money to work for you in real estate in a tax-efficient method.

On the other hand, fast cash can be your greatest choice if you need money right away to pay for critical bills or stay afloat. You could sometimes find yourself in the middle, wanting both quick cash and financial expansion.

Real estate may provide cash now, cash in the future, or a combination of the two.

Real estate may be able to assist you quickly create money in a variety of ways. This section will cover the vast majority of the choices. Often, you may make this money without using any of your own funds or credit. You would normally gain as you are setting up a deal or providing a service in return for a contract.

Plato once observed, "The defining of words is the beginning of knowledge," You must be aware of both the meanings of each term and the strategies that are now generating income for you. A greater grasp of the real estate sector may result from your ability to speak its language.

Along with wholesaling and flipping, there is also buying and resale.

Despite the fact that there are several terms or ways to express this behavior, the concept is rather simple. You persuade the owner to sell their property to you in order to flip, wholesale, or buy and resell it, and you then resell it to a new client for a greater price. You sign a contract with a buyer who will purchase the property for a higher price than what was previously agreed upon with the original owner. The money is then created in the spread, or center.

Although the concept is straightforward, it may often be difficult to get funding via this arrangement. For instance, you may, in some situations, assign your contract to a new buyer rather than closing on a house the traditional way and then selling to a different buyer after you have a contract in place with a property owner. At closing, the original owner will transfer ownership of the property to the new buyer in exchange for an assignment fee.

In other circumstances, such short sales (which will be discussed in more detail later), you would acquire the property from the prior owner, close on it using transaction money, and then right away flip it to the new buyer. Even while flipping, wholesaling, and purchasing and reselling are all terms that apply to each of these scenarios, how the spread, or the money in the middle, was earned in each instance was completely different. The concept is simple, but the repayment procedure could be more challenging. To avoid any misunderstandings, focus your attention for the time being on the current issue.

Finding properties that may be put under contract for a price that is far less than what they are now worth is essential to employing this investing technique successfully (or with favorable terms). A second buyer must also be sufficiently interested in the property to be prepared to pay you more for it than the agreed-upon price. Being the intermediary and putting the deal together might be a profitable effort if these two conditions are met.

Is it ethically improper, unethical, or otherwise harmful to be paid to buy (or put under contract) a property for less than you can immediately resell it for? Without a doubt! In fact, given the right circumstances, these alliances may be a great win-win scenario for everyone concerned. Sadly, the term "flipping" has developed a negative connotation. Actually, the detestable term "flipping" has been connected to the word "illegal." It's important to understand that a significant portion of the business has been operated on a wholesale-retail basis for decades in order to avoid any misunderstandings.

Is it against the law to buy something for a certain amount and then sell it for more? If true, the vast majority of businesses are operating according to an illegal wholesale-retail business model. Whether you buy real estate to resell it, buy it wholesale, or flip it, your business strategy is similar to that of many of the most well-known corporations in the world. You buy the same thing and then resell it to the next customer for more money. When the terms "illegal" and "flipping" are used, it alludes to a dishonest activity long practiced by the unscrupulous. When a property is sold to an ignorant buyer for far more than it is worth, it is a dubious plan.

This is how the crime is committed. In order to drastically overvalue the property in comparison to its true market value, a dishonest person first employs a second dishonest assessor. Second, the dishonest person finds a gullible and uninformed customer who would overpay for the property in order to purchase it. The purchaser then obtains a loan based on the inflated and higher-than-real value assessment. Fourth, the buyer now has a property that is worth far less than what he or she paid for it since the seller and appraiser behaved dishonestly.

As a result, the words "flipping" and "illegal" began to be used interchangeably. The issue started when dishonest people sold real estate to a buyer for far more than its fair market value. In this book, we won't discuss flipping in this way. Instead, you'll discover how to negotiate mutually beneficial arrangements that enable you to buy real estate at significant savings and resell it for its true market worth while being morally, legally, and socially compliant.

In every real estate market, there are legitimate possibilities to place houses under contract for less than their true market value. Here is a real-world case study: One of our students ran into a situation with a salesman who was really driven. In less than two months, the property owner, who owed $50,000 on a home that might be worth $150,000 or more if it were fixed up, faced foreclosure. Since the owner lacked the money to make any repairs and the tenants wouldn't let her show the home to prospective buyers, no real estate agencies were willing to help.

This seller gave up, began planning for foreclosure, furious and prepared for the worst. One of our students posted an advertising searching for motivated sellers, and that's what drew in this merchant. The parties promptly reached a written agreement wherein our student would pay $85,000 for the property. The seller was thrilled with the mutually agreed-upon assessment given that the property was in such horrible state, previous attempts to get relief had all failed, and there was only a little window before it entered foreclosure.

When the renters refused to allow anybody inside, our student immediately posted an ad looking for an all-cash investor. The buyer must be willing to acquire the property without doing a comprehensive inspection beforehand. Before the property went into foreclosure, it was revealed that a part-time investor and local doctor was willing to pay $100,000 up front for it. Consider the reasons why it was a win-win scenario for all parties and why our kid deserved to profit from it. Our student encountered a motivated merchant in need of help. Other real estate experts turned down the seller's request for assistance when she went to her. Our student resolved the seller's problem. Additionally, prior to the foreclosure, our student found a buyer willing to purchase the house in its present condition for cash (in its current condition of degradation). That kind of consumer is one that the vendor has never dealt with before. Our student deserved to gain as she created a win-win situation using her specialist financial knowledge and experience.

This was a win-win-win situation from a selling, buying, and reselling perspective. Everyone who was involved in the deal gained, even though our student ended up buying the home under contract for less than its current market value. On the other side, our student resisted taking advantage of the company owner. Because of her challenging circumstances, other real estate agents were unable to help this woman. The seller would have had to go through with a foreclosure if it weren't for the help of our pupil. She could have sold the home for $85,000 instead, which would have been $35,000 more than what she owed.

Quick cash With little to no risk (you won't lose any money if the deal doesn't work out) and little to no capital need, real estate investing allows you to create revenue quickly. On the other hand, wealth-building real estate revenues are often subject to higher taxes. In other cases, your profits can also be less than they would be if you used alternative strategies. The ideas of bulk buying, buying and reselling, and flipping have served as the foundation for the careers of many investors. It's widely used, easy to learn, and, if often used, may make you quite wealthy.

Buying, fixing, and reselling products

In contrast to the previous section, this one involves both improving the property and selling it for more money than you first purchased. This is often the image that comes to mind when most people think of real estate investing. Investment is often portrayed as buying a run-down, foreclosed property, restoring it to its former glory, and then reselling it to a first-time home buyer. This method has produced several millionaires in the past and will continue to do so because it is effective.

The ideal person to illustrate this method is a builder.

A typical builder purchases land from a developer and builds a house there. The newly finished property is then sold once again by the builder.

The developer is a real-world example of this concept. One tactic that has benefited countless real estate billionaires is buying unimproved land and developing it by constructing roads and facilities—which may need zoning changes—before selling individual lots to builders. According to an old saying, the two types of enterprises that do the best are those who "purchase whiskey by the bottle and sell it by the shot, and acquire real estate by the acre and sell it by the lot." Although purchasing, remodeling, and selling real estate may seem like the best financial plan, there are some drawbacks.

Since it involves transforming empty land into buildable lots, vacant lots into new houses, or dilapidated structures into livable dwellings, real estate renovation requires far more risk and expenditure than flipping, wholesaling, or purchasing and reselling. The purchase of the unimproved property as well as the expenditures of restoration must first be covered by funding.

Second, to enhance a property, a lot of specialized knowledge is needed. Third, most communities have regulations that must be fulfilled in order to pass inspection, regardless of whether you construct or repair anything. Fourth, when individuals are repairing the property and might be harmed while doing so, a whole new level of responsibility is introduced.

Fifth, just because you make house renovations doesn't mean the market will compensate you fairly for your labor. In this situation, developers are particularly at risk. The population may abruptly shift in the other direction when they wager on a city's expansion in one direction, just as their development project is about to be completed. As a result, constructing a home entails far more responsibility than just buying and reselling an existing one.

However, there are certain circumstances when taking a high risk offers a huge reward.

For instance, a lot of builders only make 10% on each home they construct. To invest all of that time, effort, and money in a single asset and get a return of less than 10% is risky. A few mistakes might easily destroy that profit. On the other hand, the majority of home builders profit from the sale of several houses as opposed to a single one. If they build 500 homes in a subdivision, for instance, the profit per $200,000 property multiplied by the 500 units becomes $10,000,000. That is a huge amount of cash.

When changing an unsightly house into a beautiful one, a home renovator (also known as a "rehabber") should aim for a minimum profit of 20%. This is far more cash than you would get by just selling a house for wholesale or without making any renovations. On a $200,000 home, it costs $40,000 to turn a 20% profit. That is a huge amount of cash.

A developer would pay $10,000 per acre for agricultural land and then sell four condominiums for $20,000 each. Even when particular expenditures associated with land improvements are taken into consideration, this alternative still yields a sizable return.

In any of these cases, taking up the risk of home improvement might result in a considerably greater profit.

The majority of investors do not begin with this investing plan due to the amount and level of skill required. Some individuals go closer to it, while others want to stay in the middle and work as intermediaries. On the other hand, some people choose to operate as wholesalers or flippers since they have extensive remodeling or building experience.

The finest investors are flexible and allow each transaction determine what should be done. When you discover a wonderful deal, you often have two options: accepting the risk and investing the money required to improve the property for a larger return later, or selling the property for a smaller profit and without modifications.

Commissions

Right present, commissions and other fees are the only ways to profit from real estate. A license is often necessary in order to collect this money. Real estate agents often get a 3 percent commission when they represent a buyer or seller in a transaction. These commission rates might add up quickly, and many agents make well over seven figures a year.

For whatever strange reason, the real estate investment business has been opposed to the idea of investors possessing a real estate license. They often draw attention to how it restricts and limits an investor's options. A real estate license, however, is equivalent to a permit for making money. True, it requires more of you in your commercial interactions, but isn't that what you strive for? For honest people, being held to a higher level is fantastic. You may make more money from each closing if you don't provide that money to the agent. You are entitled to request a commission refund.

One of the disadvantages is the cost and work involved in obtaining and maintaining a real estate license. It is not a cheap option. You must fulfill a number of criteria, pay hundreds of dollars in fees, fulfill continuing education requirements, get E&O insurance, and pay Realtor® dues before you can become a licensed agent. The benefit is that you could be able to earn commissions on every transaction you're presently working on, boosting your profit per deal and your ability to profit from sales unrelated to investments. In addition, you get access to the most important real estate database via the Multiple Listing Service (MLS) in your community. Unfortunately, only real estate brokers have full access to the prized MLS system.

You may be thinking, "Should I go acquire my license?" It is questionable, to put it politely. Your initial goal should be to begin investing in real estate to generate some income; after that, you may utilize some of the proceeds to seek your real estate license. Reactivating a retired license could just need one form and a little cost. If acquiring your license after retirement is so easy, you may want to do it.

If not, hold off on getting your license until you've made some cash and have some practical real estate investing experience.

There are several ways to pay bills or get commissions without working as a real estate agent. In addition to investing in real estate, some investors also work as appraisers, inspectors, or mortgage brokers. These are all possible sources of great real estate income.

The technique of "bird dogging" enables you to exchange contact details of potentially motivated sellers for a modest fee with other investors or brokers. Instead of entering into a contract, a great real estate bargain might just be entrusted to an investor or agency, who would manage the transaction from there. For a little marketing fee, a bird-business dog will simply transmit a name, phone number, or location to a more educated real estate agent. It could be a great way to quickly generate money in the real estate industry with little to no experience.

On the other hand, locating sellers who are really motivated involves more marketing expertise than negotiating a deal and placing a house under contract. A bird dog may often make considerably more money by just taking the time to understand how to negotiate with sellers, what contracts to employ, and how to properly fulfill them. Making the extra effort to execute a contract to buy the firm may be the difference between a few hundred and a few thousand dollars.

The commissions and fees associated with real estate transactions may be a useful way to boost your income. The time and money required to get and maintain the requisite permits are often the only drawbacks.

The top three real estate investing methods are listed above. You may purchase, remodel, and resell a home without making any renovations. As an alternative, you might impose a charge or commission. Now consider how investing in real estate might help you build long-term wealth.

wealth increase throughout the long run.

Investing in real estate nowadays is not only a terrific method to make money. It could also contribute to long-term monetary stability. Real estate, on the other hand, is recognized for its capacity to build long-lasting wealth. You may already know that most of the money is held in real estate. In this section, you'll discover how to leverage real estate to build a prosperous empire.

Buy now and keep it.

The most popular real estate investing tactic is this one. This strategy involves purchasing real estate, which is subsequently leased to tenants. This tactic is referred described as "classic buy-and-hold investment" It's been a fantastic way to make money. Anyone who has played Monopoly can testify to the effectiveness of real estate leasing and ownership. As has previously been said, this strategy may also be very tax-friendly, enabling you to keep more of your profits than the fast cash option discussed in the previous section.

There are three main profit margins for real estate purchases and maintenance. If the tenant pays you more each month than your expenses are, you first profit from a monthly cash flow (mortgage, taxes, insurance, maintenance, and so on). Second, it's possible that your mortgage payment includes principal, which would imply that every payment reduces the amount still owed on the property's mortgage, increasing your equity. Third, you gain from the property's appreciation since real estate often improves in value over time.

It's crucial to buy the property at a discount from its true value in order to build rapid equity and profit from the cash flow and principal pay down that follow. This is essential to carrying out the purchase and hold strategy successfully. Appreciation should be a bonus and the icing on the cake. It shouldn't be the primary variable affecting investing decisions. Many investors have lost money on real estate assets they bought in the hope of profiting from appreciation because they were unaware of this. Occasionally, supposition is used to describe this.

Investors have raised the issue of being a landlord in regard to owning and managing real estate. Some even associate landlording with clearing clogged drains at three in the morning. Property management is not disliked by everyone.

Property management is one of the most profitable sectors in the US economy (based on almost any measure of profitability). If there isn't a system in place to deal with problems as they develop or if the property's revenue flow is insufficient to cover the expenses of leasing, property management may be troublesome. However, running a property might be quite lucrative.

An Illustration from the Real World

A property owned by one of our students will now sell for around $125,000. The monthly rent is $1,000. The house is now valued at around $100,000. The whole monthly cost is $800. The principle, interest, taxes, insurance, and mortgage insurance are all paid in one payment of $800. (mortgage insurance). There is a positive cash flow of $200 as a consequence of ($1000 in rental income minus $800 in expenditures). Property management companies often charge ten percent of rental income in addition to the first month's rent when a new tenant moves in. Our student would pay a property management business $100 each month to take care of this apartment (or 50 percent of the total cash flow). As a result, there would be a positive cash flow of $100 per month. It's easy to see how property management firms may do well in this situation. A significant chunk of the deal's future profit may be represented by ten percent of the total rental income.

Utilizing the services of a property management firm could be a smart move. For managing properties, they often already have a solid leasing system in place. Since they often have links with providers like maintenance crews and eviction attorneys, an effective management system must function. They can generally handle all the issues and calls from tenants, even at three in the morning.

The fact that property management companies sometimes charge 10% of gross rental income, which may make up a significant amount of your positive cash flow, is a disadvantage. Furthermore, not all property management firms are created equal, and some lack a strong leasing base.

When a property management business generates revenue from repairs, the most destructive of all employment problems arises. The property management business may sometimes get a referral fee from the repair company for the job that has been delegated. Property managers are compelled to develop novel home improvement ideas as a result of this. Since you are responsible for all maintenance expenses, there is no practical disadvantage to charging you more. In fact, the property management company will be able to receive 10% of the total money more easily the easier it is to lease the house. In addition to getting 10% of the gross and being exempt from making any maintenance payments for the asset, they could also receive compensation for better asset maintenance.

Many investors who hired and subsequently fired their property managers were affected by this one factor. Finally, these investors learned that despite the fact that the property management company benefited from the need for repairs, it lacked the drive to choose a quality tenant who wouldn't cause harm to the property. Unfortunately, the likelihood that a tenant will do damage to a residence will affect how much money a property management company makes from the agreement.

How can a property management company predict when a difficult tenant will move in? The majority of rental applications are typically sent to the owner for final approval by property managers. In order to restrict the possibilities accessible to the owner, certain property management agencies have been known to only offer one or two possible renters. The landlord is thus forced to decide between an unreliable tenant and an unreliable renter. The property owner should next determine if the tenant is a suitable match for the property management firm. Here is another example of how to ask the barber if you need a haircut. A excellent tenant for a landlord could be a difficulty for a property management company, which is the problem. It could be in the best interests of the property management business to re-lease often, given that each one charges one-third of the initial month's price. Sadly, a property management company's financial objectives can not align with those of a property owner.

Should you utilize a property management firm to manage your home? In the last scenario, our student is in charge of looking after his own property. Why? This student, first and foremost, has a great system in place for managing rental properties, from how to quickly identify suitable tenants to how to manage complaints about blocked toilets at three in the morning. Second, he already has all the vendors necessary to run a successful management system, from the eviction lawyer to the maintenance worker. The student who is gratis watching after the property is thus worth $100 per month.

However, there are a number of excellent property management firms out there. If the property is far from the owner, the owner lacks a system, or there is no personnel in place, it is much better to hire a property management company. A property management company that you own, run by your rules, and employ your people is the greatest of all possible worlds.

The cost to acquire and maintain real estate may vary greatly depending on the kind of property. Single-family houses could be relatively easy to sell if a tenant moves out and you want to take advantage of your equity. On the other hand, renting single-family houses may be pricey if a tenant defaults on payments or the property is left vacant since there is no means to fill the vacancy and you have to pay significant holding costs until the property is re-leased.

Examples of properties that make money and include extra units to cover your monthly expenses in the event of a vacancy are duplexes (2 units), triplexes (3 units), quads (4 units), and apartment complexes. Properties that provide income, however, may be more difficult to sell and may appreciate more slowly. This is because income-producing properties are often valued based on how much money they produce, unlike single-family homes, which are valued largely on what the market would pay for them. Single-family homes are the residential properties that have the broadest appeal and appreciate more quickly than investment properties. Rental costs often don't rise as quickly as real estate costs do. Some investors decide to buy and hold single-family homes because they can sell them for more money.

Investors in income-producing properties value the steady cash flow and flexibility to add additional rental units to meet any vacancies, particularly during times of low vacancy. You'll identify the issue on which you wish to focus your efforts as you spend. Investors often hold both income-producing assets and single-family homes. Some individuals go on to run bigger apartment complexes due to the economies of scale that may be gained by having a large number of units all in one area with a full-time, onsite manager. One of the many advantages of owning an apartment complex greater than a certain size is the chance to hire an on-site manager to keep an eye on things. To receive outstanding service at a far lower total cost, you may pay the person a salary rather than the standard 10 percent per unit.

However, putting all of your eggs in one basket might be fatal if it falls. Smart investors will employ 1031 exchanges to merge their single-family homes, duplexes, and quads into one huge apartment building. At first glance, everything seems to be in order. When economic circumstances change, their apartment building stops making money. Their basket begins to disintegrate. Because an investor puts all of their financial eggs in one basket, their level of financial security depends on how that property performs over the long term. What is the conclusion? Keep your eggs from being all in one basket.

The secret to successfully owning and managing real estate is to be very careful when purchasing residences. If you choose the right property and take care of it, it may be a profitable and rewarding investment. The process might be difficult and irritating if you purchase or maintain the property incorrectly.

Some analysts think that a bad investment may ultimately provide a return even if you purchase real estate wrongly. As you learned from the Yale lecturer and the example of Baytown, Texas, this is not always the case. If you have access to people who have learnt through a lifetime of real estate ownership experiences, you may be able to make better decisions and achieve more success.

In certain situations, the government could be a landlord's greatest ally. The government may repay property owners for all or a part of their monthly rent payments via a welfare-related program known as Section 8. Payments are paid on time each month since, as of the time of writing, the government has not yet declared bankruptcy. The government gives a predetermined amount for each bed the property has in accordance with Section 8. (and any of its local variants). A part of the monthly rent may be paid by the tenant in certain circumstances, while the whole amount may be covered by the government in others.

The majority of Section 8 homeowners profit from the government covering their whole monthly payment. To be eligible for the program, the property must fulfill a strict set of requirements stated by the Section 8 agency. When a rental is accepted by Section 8 tenants, the owner may relax knowing that rent payments will always be made on time by Uncle Sam (assuming the government-issued checks are valid and do not bounce due to inadequate cash). Section 8 could be a wise alternative for investors who want the benefits of long-term ownership and holding without the headaches of thinking about their monthly rent payment. There are some drawbacks despite all of the seeming benefits. First off, Section 8 houses may have maintenance issues since the tenant is not particularly motivated to keep the property in excellent shape. The renter has no title to the property, particularly if the government pays the whole monthly rent. The second is that "those in the free seats hiss first." according to an old Chinese proverb. Customers complain more when they are charged less in business, which may seem surprising. Typically, a landlord would find it far simpler to manage a tenant renting a good property for $8,000 per month than a Section 8 tenant receiving $800 per month from the government. Most often, a tenant calling section 8 property management at three in the morning has a minor concern. The solution is a superb property management system. A Section 8 investor must also be well-versed in the particular regulations, constraints, and complexities of the local Section 8 program where the property is located as they may vary from state to state and even county to county. The downside of increased administrative costs balances the benefit of practically assured income that comes with government-sponsored housing.

Purchase, Control, Rent-to-Own, and Sale Upon Agreement

Real estate investors have worked very hard to lessen the risks of traditional buy-and-hold investing while still enjoying the benefits. In other words, they have attempted to have their cake and drink it too. They are looking for a tenant who is committed to paying rent on time each month and who will also take care of and cover any potential maintenance concerns. As a consequence, "sell on terms,""rent to own," or "lease with a purchase option" a revolutionary financial technique, was developed.

Since "rent to own" homes are rare, single-family homes are the most prevalent kind of income-producing asset. The tenant is now referred to as a "tenant buyer," distinguishing them from other renters since they are no longer tenants. They should be more inclined to pay their obligations on time and take care of any maintenance issues that emerge because they will ultimately be the owner.

Numerous uses may be made of this idea. While being maintained by other investors, the house is just leased to the tenant buyer, who has the possibility to purchase the home after a year or two, while other investors transfer ownership of the property to the tenant buyer and then accrue mortgage payments much like a bank. Some investors take this idea a step further by leasing with the option to buy the property from the original owner and then re-leasing to a new tenant buyer, a procedure known as a sandwich lease option. Given that every state has a distinct set of limitations, what works in one state could not work in another. The most important thing is to comprehend the concept rather than getting bogged down in the particulars of creative finance (which we'll explore in the subsequent chapter). You locate a tenant buyer who prefers to buy the property than renting it out to tenants. Even if the change is little, it has a significant effect.

This approach may include all of the profit margins seen in traditional buy-and-hold investments, the chance to get an upfront, non-refundable option payment from the tenant (as opposed to a refundable deposit), or a down payment if the house is being sold subject to restrictions. Furthermore, you can stand to gain handsomely if the tenant buyer really closes on a deal to buy the property at the end of the option period.

This sell on a rent to own basis technique is often used in conjunction with the buy, renovate, and resale tactics by rehabbers. This is a terrific investing approach for three reasons. First off, if you offer a buyer favorable terms, you may be able to sell a house for more cash than you would on the open market to a bidder who secures their own financing. By forgoing sales commissions while selling a home on the open market, you might save up to 6%. Third, the IRS counts the profit as long-term capital gains rather than ordinary income if the property is retained for at least a year, which might result in large tax savings.

But with all of these benefits, there must be some drawbacks, right? Selling a home means permanently giving up the possibility to earn from that asset for passionate buy-and-hold investors. Real estate investors who are knowledgeable and creative, however, might dispute that assertion by noting that only around 20% of all tenants really make use of the decision they made to acquire the property. As a consequence, properties that are for rent with a buy option are seldom sold.

Furthermore, this method might be difficult to implement for any property other than a single-family house since apartment tenants are not often interested in buying apartment complexes. Some investors believe that people care about own possessions more than the items they borrow from others. In other words, renters who believe they are the owners of the property are more likely to do harm than tenants who believe they are renting it.

Renting your house to a tenant buyer under a rent-to-own agreement may often provide you the best of both worlds in terms of long-term wealth growth.

Even while there are creative ways to lessen some of the risks associated with owning real estate, you are still working with people, and people don't always keep their word. When you purchase real estate, you are accepting a huge obligation, in contrast to the fast cash approach of investing, which enables you to get in and out as soon as possible. Even if the renter or tenant buyer fails on their obligations, you are still liable for making payments and maintaining the property.

It has been said that entering into a real estate transaction is often far easier than exiting one. To lessen your chances of running into problems, be selective and only invest in initiatives that have a high degree of error tolerance.

They now have a ton of stock that is accessible, excellent cash flow forecasts, favorable financing terms, or all three. Many people have become rich via real estate investment and rental income; it may be your ticket to financial freedom. It does, however, offer a special set of challenges that you must consider in your efforts.

Without regard for accomplishment, ambitious people often think that acquiring more real estate will help them succeed. Instead of just buying more real estate, the goal should be to purchase excellent real estate assets. Having fewer goods and managing them well is preferable than having more items and making poor purchase decisions. Develop your real estate holdings gradually and cautiously. It will last for a very long time.

Chapter Two

Motives for Thinking About Real Estate Investment

Why should you consider investing in real estate? There are, after all, several strategies to increase your income in life. According to statistics recently issued by the Internal Revenue Service, the nation's main personal financial institution, real estate makes up the bulk of US taxpayers' personal wealth. Have you ever considered starting your own company, going into business for yourself, or exercising independent judgment? The IRS lists being an entrepreneur and establishing your own firm as the two paths to become independently affluent in your lifetime. Opportunity seekers could spend a lot of time investigating the most effective ways to make money. If you are a member of this group, you may put off starting your education. Starting a real estate firm offers the best potential of financial success. Real estate is the ideal investment, which is one of the factors contributing to its success.

Income.

The regular, tax-favored income that real estate may provide you is referred to as cash flow. A renter may be leased real estate. The rent you get from that renter, plus with any maintenance and management costs, may eventually cover your mortgage, leaving you with a reliable source of income. Despite the fact that there are alternative assets that might give dependable income, such as bonds and dividend-paying shares, real estate often produces a bigger quantity of income and is more tax advantageous than bond coupon payments or stock dividends.

Depreciation.

This phrase is utilized for tax considerations, therefore real estate investors should be aware of it. Consider the lifespan of a t-shirt to help you understand the notion of depreciation. It deteriorates after being used and cleaned for a while. Even while you may have few that have lasted decades, the average t-shirt will probably only last a few years. To determine how much you would pay in taxes on your real estate investment, the IRS set the life span of a residential rental property at 27 12 years. The IRS has recognised that a property's structure, not only the soil, deteriorates with time. Does a well-kept home simply fall apart after 27 and a half years? Obviously not. The amount you paid for the home (without the land) may be depreciated over a 27-year period to determine how much you would owe the IRS.

Example.

You invest $100,000 on a one-family house with a $10,000 land value. That implies that your tax base is $90,000 (the amount at which you acquired the building). Depreciation is calculated as $90,000 divided by 12 years, yielding a $3,272.73 tax benefit every year. If the same single family house generates positive cash flow of $270 per month, or $3,000 per year, you may be able to avoid paying income taxes on the $270 per month you were bringing in by deducting $3,240 in depreciation from that asset! This explains why the rental income from real estate is so tax-efficient.

Why does the government continue to provide this exemption to real estate investors in the face of tax rises and discriminatory tax laws? Real estate investment is being promoted by the government. They urge you to invest in real estate.

Equity.

You may choose to pay less for real estate when you buy it than what the market would bear. Equity is the difference between what you spent and what something is worth when you get a good bargain. "In real estate, you make your money when you buy," goes the proverb. When you purchase a home for a modest part of its market value, you gain quick equity. Publicly traded equities, on the other hand, are purchased at market value. Regardless of whether the market is undervaluing or overvaluing the stock at the time of acquisition, the price paid is what the market will provide for it. On the other hand, if you invest in real estate, you may purchase a house for less than market value and then sell it not long after for a lot more money. We practice this very often.

Appreciation.

Data show that residential real estate has typically kept pace with inflation during the last century. Residential real estate prices have risen in many regions far faster than inflation. Appreciation is a financial benefit of real estate ownership, not its primary driver, for wise and knowledgeable investors. Given how difficult it is to forecast the future, purchasing real estate based on the other aspects outlined above is a far better option than placing a wager on whether or not a property will appreciate in value. You can only gain from a property's appreciation if you own it. As a result, if you buy as much real estate as you can and take good care of it, your prospects of profiting from appreciation may be at their maximum. And be grateful if it comes your way.

Leverage.

Leverage is used while taking out a loan to purchase real estate. Most financial organizations in the world, including banks, mortgage lenders, hedge funds, mutual funds, pension funds, insurance providers, and private individuals, want to lend you money so that you may purchase real estate. A large portion of them make their income by lending you money for property. There are many various sorts of lenders for real estate, from those that only provide funds depending on the market worth of the property to others who merely need excellent credit, a sizeable sum of money, and a strong loan application. Leverage, for instance, allows you to purchase an asset for $100,000 with just $10,000 of your own funds if you put down a $10,000 deposit on a $100,000 property. The capacity to borrow money to acquire real estate is referred to as leverage since it allows you to buy more property at a cheaper price.

Real estate is without a doubt the finest investment. This is only one of many compelling factors for real estate. Here are a few more elements that might help real estate investing become for you the best company or investment vehicle.

Anyone, regardless of age, background, or race, may invest in real estate. You are the ideal age, neither too young nor too old (although you must be 18 years old to own property.) You are on an even playing field with everyone else, regardless of where you are from, how old you are, or what nation you are from.

Real estate investment does not need a resume. No matter where you went to college, how many jobs you've had, if you have any professional skills, or the color and texture of the paper used for your CV, none of these things matter. Investors that are successful come from a range of backgrounds. You are not less than just because you don't have a better degree of education. My role model never attended college. A college degree or other post-college credential is also not a disadvantage. No matter how impressive your qualifications are, everyone is on an equal footing.

When buying or selling real estate, there are alternatives to paying cash or utilizing credit. This book will teach you a number of strategies that will enable you to acquire real estate for the goal of creating long-term wealth without having to make any down payments or take out any loans, in addition to making quick money. It goes without saying that having cash on hand and/or strong credit can increase an investor's real estate investing opportunities, but as you can see from my personal experience, it is feasible to start from nothing.

Housing is a basic human need. Everyone needs a roof over their head, as the phrase goes. Residential real estate investment will be the main topic of this book. Single family homes, duplexes, condominiums, townhouses, apartments, co-ops, and a wide variety of other housing alternatives are available. Contrary to many other companies and investments, real estate offers a service that everyone needs: shelter.

Real estate may be found almost everywhere, even your own home. It's a prevalent fallacy among immigrants that real estate investment doesn't work where they live. Non-sense! A chance is there in front of your face. Your own garden could contain diamonds. In fact, you'll be surprised at how much money you can make with real estate in your local region if you understand and put the techniques and concepts discussed in this book to use. Whether you are aware of it or not, every day as you travel, you are passing by real estate chances. Real estate prospects are many, especially in your own neighborhood.

You might decide to make a local or global real estate investment. There are other possibilities than what is around you. Although you may purchase and sell real estate anywhere, we suggest beginners start by doing so in a familiar area.

You may potentially earn money in both up and down markets. Certain real estate marketing tactics work well in an increasing market, while in a contracting market, other marketing tactics work better. Real estate investing might be successful in any market.

To get started as a real estate investor, you don't need a lot of tools. You can get started right away if you already have a phone, printer, and computer. You are permitted to work anywhere, including at home, at a coffee shop, or even in your vehicle! vs beginning almost any other kind of company, which often calls for commercial space, a lease, staff, inventory, and equipment, among other things.

The majority of ventures with a similar likelihood of generating financial returns are considerably more challenging to commence than real estate investment. A board of directors, a thorough business strategy, or even the use of venture money are not necessities. Your financial strategy might simply be a hurriedly scrawled note on a napkin.

Real estate investing does not need you to spend all of your time on it. In your spare time, you can invest in a side business. Although it's not required, you could find that you really like it and wish to pursue it full-time. In other words, you do not necessarily need to leave your day job to try your hand at real estate investment.

With the limited free time you have, you could invest.

The two biggest advantages could be the chance to live the lifestyle you've always desired and becoming very wealthy via real estate. The list of the world's wealthiest individuals makes it clear that many of them made their fortunes in real estate.

Many of the residents in the most expensive homes in your neighborhood earned or preserved their fortune via real estate. In addition, many of the financially independent individuals you see on the street have real estate expertise.

So, if investing in real estate is so great, why isn't everyone doing it? One may reflect. That is a very excellent question. Real estate has several restrictions on entrance (a fancy business term to describe what makes a business difficult for competitors to break into).

Real estate investment takes a high level of competence, just like any other business. This skill is seldom taught in schools. The majority of individuals have no idea how to invest in real estate. In addition, the educational process requires both study and application. Developing a thorough understanding of real estate investment requires both absorbing educational materials and putting what you learn into practice and experiencing it in the real world, much as high school chemistry did when you had the lecture and then the laboratory. Even by reading about them, certain ideas and concepts might be hard to comprehend. Go outdoors so you can see it for yourself.

When making real estate investments, patience is required. The society in which we live values quick gratification. Real estate does not provide instant satisfaction. Usually, the work you put in a few months ago is now beginning to pay off. When they are just a few days away from receiving a sizeable reward, some half-hearted would-be investors quit up. This phenomena has often occurred to me. Some individuals just don't have the endurance to wait for their real estate investment endeavors to produce noticeable results.

Real estate investment is really the beginning of your own company. Any business owner will also tell you that a company's success determines its financial benefits. The ordinary method that individuals get paid in life, which is based on performance and paid either hourly or on a salary basis, contrasts strongly with this. Business owners are compensated based on the accomplishments their company makes in the marketplace. Successful company owners and salaried workers think quite differently.

Since most individuals must retrain their thinking to that of a successful company owner, beginning a business is more psychologically hard than physically difficult for them.

Real estate is unquestionably the best vehicle for achieving financial success. You must have the skills and mental ability required to run a successful real estate firm in order to take advantage of the numerous possibilities that real estate offers. Developing an attitude of investment and training yourself in the particular disciplines that will assure success are the two real estate-related topics that the rest of this book will concentrate on.

Consider your options as an investment.

Pain and pleasure are the two things in life that drive us the most. We base our choices on two things: the pleasure we anticipate deriving from them and the agony we anticipate they will hopefully save us. If you desire to spend every day on the beach, surrounded by the sun and sand, that may be your why. That is a wonderful example of pursuing pleasure. On the other hand, you can be motivated by a desire to never again struggle to make ends meet. That serves as an example of the desire to be pain-free. This concept may seem straightforward, yet it really represents how our brains function.

By putting this simple yet very useful concept into practice, you will gain knowledge of a whole new universe. You could learn new techniques for motivating yourself. For instance, the paralyzing effects of worry are felt by most novice investors. They are hesitant to get into a contract, meet a motivated seller, and, among other things, want non-refundable earnest money from a buyer. The issue is that suggestions often promote positive thinking. In your endeavor to tackle your fear, just thinking positively could lead you to lose sight of reality. There's no need to run away from life's facts. On the other hand, fear may really be good for us. Fear is an excellent teacher and guide.

Why not channel fear into motivation rather than suppress it? Instead of thinking about what to say to the homeowner, tell yourself, "If I don't call this person, it may cost me $30,000, which would severely upset me, and I need the money," The urge to enjoy pleasure is far less than the need to prevent misery. Most individuals would battle far harder to reclaim $20,000 if it were stolen from them than they would to slowly accumulate $20,000 in savings. The drive to stay away from suffering is far greater than the motivation to enjoy it. Make use of this understanding to spur you on to action.

Start considering all the things you stand to lose if you do nothing, especially when concern starts to impede or even paralyze your investment path. Consider it carefully until you begin to sense the agony that would result if you took no action. For instance, some novices could find it upsetting and unsettling to ask customers for non-refundable earnest money (and, unfortunately, some seasoned investors). Ironically, an investor would never ask for non-refundable earnest money again after they have lost money on an investment as a result of a buyer breaking a contract and leaving them high and dry.

Here's how to use the desire to avoid suffering to persuade a new investor to give a potential buyer non-refundable earnest money. They might think, "If I don't require non-refundable earnest money from this buyer, I'll possibly allow this buyer to back out of the deal scot-free, costing me $37,000 in addition to the time I've spent getting this deal to this point, not to mention harming the homeowner who is depending on me to help him." Do you see how suffering and apprehension may be utilized to influence your decisions? If you manage your pain and fear instead of ignoring it, your life will change.

All attention is on you.

Have you ever encountered someone who had the knowledge to act morally but choose not to? Is it possible that you have sometimes behaved in such manner? If that's the case, how did you avoid taking action while being fully aware of what was required? The solution is hidden in your subconscious.

Although you were aware of how to accomplish it, you didn't because your brain forbade you from doing that action since you had previously connected or associated suffering with it. Positive and negative emotions are intricately linked to our ideas in our brains. Every action you do is continually assigned a "pleasure" or "pain." label by your mind.

For instance, many new real estate investors are nervous about speaking with property sellers. Before calling the owner to learn more about the person's position, many inexperienced investors would first get in their car, go to the property, inspect the outside, study the neighborhood, come home, and then do a ton of online research on the property. The interesting part is that the home owner could not even want to sell or they can have inflated expectations. This takes a lot of time, effort, and money. Why would anybody in their right mind spend all that time, effort, and money if they could just pick up the phone and ask a few simple questions? This person suffered more pain as a result of that one simple phone call than they did as a result of the time, money, and effort they spent. People will go to great efforts to avoid pain as opposed to desiring it.

To expand on the preceding example, this person considered phoning the property owner to be the most unpleasant action. Driving and doing research online were both well within his or her capabilities. Your financial comfort level won't change over time. If you want to excel in life, you'll need to continuously push yourself outside your comfort zone.

Your financial comfort level won't change over time.

What happens if they are unable to operate a motor vehicle? Everybody's level of comfort varies. Therefore, the call would be far more useful than the drive. What if they were having issues utilizing the Internet? Then, making a phone call would have been far more useful than searching online.

All of the exercises in this book ought to be within your comfort zone. If not, make a mental commitment to go beyond your comfort zone. You might do this by improving your phone-calling tactics. Using a computer to arrange your company online rather than in paper files is one example of how to do this. The list may never end.

You must be willing to push beyond your restrictions. Permitting yourself to consider venturing outside of your comfort zone Why? The Why question is brought up once again. If you have previously determined your Why, you need to be able to explain why stepping outside of your comfort zone is so crucial. Your biggest breakthroughs will occur when you go from actions that are outside of your comfort zone to behaviors that are even more outside of your comfort zone.

Attitude.

A successful real estate investor has a certain attitude. Each exchange is seen as a test, with the results serving as a lesson. This approach creates a failure-unafraid mentality. Nothing is wasted to an investor with the appropriate mentality; the expression "Well, that was a waste of time" is never uttered. Every conversation is an experiment, and every outcome is a learning opportunity.

This tactic, nevertheless, does not necessarily result in a happy or satisfying encounter. The fact is that great investors sometimes go through difficult times, and instead of trying to escape the pain, they endure it to avoid having to learn the lesson again. If a test yields a result that wasn't what you expected, you shouldn't assume it's a negative sign. You'll subsequently understand that, despite how bothersome and painful it may appear now, the lesson you learned was really very important for your ability to clinch the subsequent business that came your way.

Being grateful is one attribute that excellent investors have. They are grateful for the chance to make investments. They value the information and life lessons they have learned. When challenges happen, they see them as chances for growth rather than as something to be griped about.

Action always comes before analysis.

Fear is the fundamental reason why so many people remain inactive. Fear of the future, fear of failure, and fear of stepping beyond one's comfort zone are all contributing factors. The prospect of doing nothing at all should terrify them the most! When starting a new activity, keep in mind that errors are inevitable. You may learn more rapidly by making more errors. Then being idle should be your greatest fear. What is the most common regret of the top real estate investors, in actuality? They wished they had begun working on it sooner.

Analysis paralysis is a common problem for inexperienced investors. The individual keeps evaluating rather than acting until they are completely motionless. It comes from a fear of making an error. These folks study a lot of books and go to plenty of seminars, but they never do any business. They persuade themselves that they won't start investing until they are certain and knowledgeable enough. Many would-be investors fail to realize that unless they take action, they won't have enough knowledge about real estate to feel confident. A book won't give you the confidence that comes from understanding what you're doing. It will occur if anything is done.

Continuous learning is crucial for long-term real estate success, but only if you put what you're learning into practice. Investors constantly develop novel strategies, networks, and investment ideas. They will never be fully informed about all facets of real estate. As a result, waiting to act until one is certain that they know exactly what to do might leave them paralyzed for the rest of their lives. Unexpectedly, we've discovered that investors who have less information but are less hesitant to try and act yield outcomes that are far better and earlier than those who have a lot of expertise but take less action. Analysis is ineffective compared to taking action.

Commitment.

According to a quote attributed to Sam Walton, the founder of Wal-Mart, the biggest retailer in the world, "like any over-night success, it's normally 20 years in the making." He argued that perseverance is essential for success. One thing that all successful real estate investors have in common is that they persisted until they were successful. Is that not simple?

If you want to be sure that your objectives are achieved, you must be prepared to make a serious and legally binding commitment to follow through until you succeed. Don't tell yourself stuff like, "I'll give this three months." however. If it succeeds, I'll continue to do it. If it is unsuccessful, I will attempt another approach. That is the very antithesis of dedication, and it ensures failure in whatever you do. Instead, if you're serious about succeeding in real estate, you must commit to persevering through it to the end. "till." is the crucial word in this assertion. That dedication is important.

In a world with plenty of beginnings, you want to be a finisher. Once your endeavor is complete and you feel successful in it, you may decide to reevaluate. That is the way successful people think. They persuade themselves to think, "I'll do this for as long as it takes until I succeed, and then I'll re-evaluate."

If beginning a real estate investment firm is something you're passionate about, make a commitment to see it through to the end. You are well on your way to greatness if you can make such a commitment to your future, your loved ones, and yourself.

You may instantly follow through on your new promise after reading this book!

The idea of possibility thinking may be used in any situation.

The real money is generated when investors can pinpoint at least one of these factors, and successful investors are aware that projects often fail for a number of reasons. Possibility I refer to it as thinking. Ask yourself, "How can it work?" rather than concentrating on the reasons why something won't work. Instead of merely thinking optimistically, which may overlook reality and potentially impede progress, possibility thinking entails examining the icy, stern realities of a problem before coming up with innovative solutions. Here's an easy way to get your capacity for possibility thinking going. Replace "no" with "yes, but." the next time you're negotiating or making a choice with someone else. You'll be inspired to think more creatively and identify more solutions to issues as a result. You must perceive potential if you want to be a successful real estate investor.

You can because you have the capacity to overcome them. Avoid making the regretful error of letting a four-foot obstruction stand in the way of your goals.

Repetition

The foundation of skill is consistent practice. You must continually practice everything you want to become excellent at. Repetition is the key to mastery, regardless of how well you believe you learn or how quickly you think you can retain new material.

You'll discover that reading the same content more than once could be really beneficial. When your point of view shifts, you'll also become aware of ideas and concepts that you hadn't previously considered.

As you continually practice the techniques you've learned in this book, they'll soon become second nature to you, becoming ingrained in your subconscious mind. Real estate investment then becomes so simple you could do it while you were sleeping. The minds of the most successful investors are inherently programmed to think like investors. For something to be mastered, practice is required.

Humility.

The investor's mental arsenal should include humility. There is a long list of famous individuals who have fallen from lofty heights due to ego and conceit. Being sensitive and listening more than speaking are requirements for humility. It necessitates putting one's ego aside and abstaining from passing judgment. Being modest helps you avoid becoming agitated or stressed easily. It hints that you are adaptable, accepting of change, and aware that not everything will go as to plan.

Being modest might help you to be open to new ideas and learn from your failures. It could be challenging for someone who believes they have all the answers to let new thoughts into their head. Some have compared this technique to having a cup that is overflowing. Your cup has to be completely empty. You must make room for fresh ideas. Those that go into real estate with full cups fail terribly. Those with empty cups offer themselves the chance to finally develop and discover new things.

If you have humility, you won't blame others for your business failures. Instead, you assume personal accountability for the situation. This is how you become a great investor: by accepting responsibility for your accomplishments (or failures) and improving as a result. Being modest does not imply being young. Actually, humility is an indication of power. You could be a leader who remains composed under stress and is aggressive while yet being humble. There is a delicate line between self-assurance and vanity, between knowing oneself and knowing all there is to know about oneself. Successful investors are self-assured but humble.

Chapter Three

The makeup of the real estate sector

Many real estate investors begin by purchasing a residence to live in for a period, after which they purchase a second property and rent out the first one. Some have discovered that a different strategy for obtaining rental properties is the most effective for hastening the process of turning becoming a real estate investor.

We'll swiftly look at some of the most popular approaches to buying investment properties or engaging in the real estate market, and we'll tell you whether or not you should adopt them. Foreclosures, REOs, and lease opportunities are the first types of properties we look at. We look at a few additional, even stranger methods for obtaining real estate below market value, such as probate sales and auctions. Other passive real estate investment options, in addition to REITs, covered in this article include limited partnerships, notes and trust deeds, and triple net properties.

Locating Foreclosed and Bank-Owned Homes.

Do you find it more feasible to purchase real estate at retail or wholesale prices? Without a doubt, "Wholesale!" Both the stock market and the real estate market are examples of when it makes sense to "buy low, sell high" A repossessed home or other REO property is one of the finest methods to increase your chances of receiving a reasonable return on your investment. Although they carry a higher level of risk, these investments often provide higher returns than regular purchases.

There are other investors looking for great offers in your local real estate market, and they are also looking for good deals. Wealthy real estate investors are almost guaranteed to seize this opportunity. Anyone looking to purchase one or two foreclosed houses in their neighborhood may be surprised to learn that they are up against large, seasoned Wall Street venture companies with tens of millions of dollars to invest in collections of subprime mortgages or foreclosed homes.

To put it simply, foreclosures are homes whose owners have neglected to make payments on their loans or otherwise violated the conditions of their loans, forcing the lender to seize ownership and legal possession of the home in order to collect any money owing to them (or foreclose and take title). Despite the fact that a real estate foreclosure is more formal legally and takes longer, it is equivalent to a lender taking back control of a vehicle from an owner who has missed monthly auto payments.

After the foreclosure procedure is over, the lender receives title to the property and becomes the actual owner. Since the lender is in charge of its maintenance and administration, asset managers in the internal real estate owned (REO) department get ownership of the property. The majority of lenders hire local property management companies to look over the property, fix any urgent issues that arise, and basically run the property until the lender can sell it, which typically takes place within a few months unless the borrower has redemption rights. Asset managers may be in charge of day-to-day property management internally, but the majority of lenders do not. The owned real estate operations department of several big lenders, notably Bank of America, is in charge of managing repossessed assets (OREOs). Whatever the moniker, the savvy investor in real estate who is prepared to put in the time and effort required to do careful due diligence in order to identify the rare diamonds in the rough will be rewarded.

It is usual practice to sell these properties for a price that is as near to their appraised value as is practicable after promptly restoring them. However, given the high number of foreclosures in many parts of the nation, lenders could find it difficult to sell these homes. Robert claims that in the hope that the market would turn around and the lenders will be able to recoup a substantial portion of their loan payments, local property management businesses are being hired to clean the properties and rent them out for one to three years. When more private lenders join the market, this is especially true.

It is a good practice even if public lenders, like most banks, may not always have the choice to maintain these nonperforming assets on their books due to regulatory restrictions. The recovery will happen gradually over many years and result in a consistent supply of rental properties at fair rates as different lenders start to sell some of the assets they have bought. However, real estate investors may notice fewer fire-sale offers in the near future.

Make sure you've done your homework before considering REOs and foreclosures:

Determine the property's physical condition and the approximate cost of any required repairs by inspecting it. Be careful to get rid of any potential environmental hazards.

To see whether there are any current tax liens or other encumbrances, verify the property's title.

Evaluate the property, establish a goal price, and a clear maximum offer in order to prevent being swept up in the thrill of bidding and overpaying.

Foreclosures.

The process through which a lender takes possession of a property when a loan is not repaid is referred to as "foreclosure" The two high-risk errors that lead to foreclosure among homeowners most often are:

- violation of the terms of the mortgage payment agreement
- Homeowners who had little to no down payment and 100% financing were literally living on the brink of bankruptcy.
- When refinancing, keep your debt to a minimum.

Refinancing gave homeowners access to record low interest rates, which were available in the early to mid-2000s, a period of sharply rising real estate values throughout the country. As long as you don't borrow excessive amounts, refinancing is OK. However, some lenders advertised loans with interest rates of 110 to 120 percent, advising homeowners to use all of their equity and even more to pay off their debt. The current tendency toward loans with minimal supporting documents or reported income has also played a role in the current real estate meltdown.

It was believed that because these people were borrowing money against potential future equity, real estate values would continue to rise. On the other hand, a little setback, such as losing a job or source of income, being very sick, having a funeral, or getting divorced, might result in a few missed mortgage payments and eventually a foreclosure. The housing market has turned against them as a result of this. Due to their excessive debt loads, millions of homeowners risked financial catastrophe in the late 2000s. Even while some people were unable to pay their mortgages, others choose to leave properties that were worth less than the amount owed.

Failure to comply with other loan requirements, such as skipping mortgage payments, is another cause of property foreclosure. For instance, failing to maintain the property in excellent physical condition or having insufficient insurance coverage are both negative. Absent landlords are unable to effectively manage their properties while they are away. An excellent property manager regularly inspects and visits their tenants. Working remotely is insufficient to reach this level of engagement.

For out-of-town investors, these sorts of foreclosures, which are relatively common, rank among the most tempting real estate investment prospects in places like Las Vegas and Phoenix. Even if you are not at one of these markets, you could find some fantastic deals. Like previous investors, don't buy houses that are out of your price range.

The owners wish to stay clear of serious issues. Foreclosures may occur when the present owner of a property decides to ignore major recurring problems rather than solve them. Top of the list concerns often include environmental threats and serious physical issues (such as cracked slabs) that may need repairs that would be more expensive than the property is worth.

Many foreclosure homes also fell into this category since many real estate investors believed the market was so strong that nearly any property they acquired would improve in value over the next few years. Time that may have been the case in certain markets for a while, investors who made hasty purchases of homes often learned that they had made "white elephants," purchases of homes that they couldn't recoup their expenditures (or even rent out to cover their carrying costs).

Learn about the different foreclosure processes that are often employed in your state before you begin looking at foreclosure properties. For more information, speak with your preferred lender, real estate agent, real estate attorney, or title business representative. One of two groupings might be applied to your state:

The loan is made in a jurisdiction where deeds of trust are frequent, therefore the title to the property is held in the name of a trustee or other third party when a loan is made there. If the loan installments are not paid on time or the loan is in default for any other reason, the trustee may be able to foreclose on the property or take it back. In places where deeds of trust are used, foreclosures may be completed in 60 to 120 days without a court judgment. This sort of foreclosure is referred to as "Nonjudicial foreclosure"

Examine your knowledge of legislative and judicial initiatives at the federal, state, and even local levels. In California, for instance, judges and legislators have been active in extending deadlines to allow debtors additional time to prevent foreclosure.

A mortgage state does not choose a trustee or third party, in contrast to other states. When a mortgage is in default owing to nonpayment or any other infraction, the mortgage holder must pursue legal remedies in court, including judicial foreclosure, which may take some time.

It's easy to locate a foreclosure property. Regardless of whether you live in a deed of trust or a mortgage state, the filing of a Notice of Default (NOD) or the filing of a court foreclosure action are both public records in your state. The local legal newspaper of record must publish further public notice of the upcoming foreclosure auction. State-by-state differences exist in how long passes between a book's release and its sale. The events leading up to and involving foreclosure are tracked by a large number of title agencies and real estate firms. You should sign up for one of the local businesses that provides you this information daily or weekly through email or fax since getting it on your own takes time and is inconvenient. This information has been submitted to the county recorder or a comparable office and is public record.

There are four phases to the usual foreclosure procedure, providing prospective purchasers of a home in the midst of the process four choices. Mastering these steps, as well as the tactics or negotiating points that must be used at each stage to persuade the owner or lender, is necessary for one of the most effective techniques for buying real estate at below-market or wholesale prices, which we will go over in more detail in the following sections.

Pre-foreclosure.

Every prospective foreclosure occurs when the owner fails to make a debt service payment or, as was stated before, when the lender notifies the owner in writing that a loan requirement or term is not being complied with. Pre-foreclosure occurs prior to the lender filing a Notice of Default, which initiates the whole foreclosure process. For purchasers, the time period between the start of the legal foreclosure process and the start of the sale is crucial: You can get an edge over the competition by spotting homes where the owner has neglected to make mortgage payments or has otherwise broken the terms of her loan before the competition does. It is difficult to track down and pursue these enraged property owners. This is the moment to offer the property owner a plan that would allow her to leave the property while also safeguarding her credit so that, should the need arise, she may purchase a house in the future. Any homeowner who has fallen behind on their mortgage will additionally need funds for moving and relocation expenses. It may be essential to comprehend the objectives of the owner and lender in order to develop an investment strategy that satisfies everyone's needs and enables you to buy a property before it is actively promoted on the local multiple listing service.

A default notice.

The filing of a Notice of Default marks the start of the official legal process of foreclosure. Whether or whether the owner was worried when he initially started skipping loan payments, the Notice of Default should be taken seriously.

When a homeowner receives a Notice of Default, she is aware that her lender has started the official process of regaining ownership of the property and may feel pressured to sell. Many homeowners who are facing foreclosure are unaware that their already bad financial situation might become considerably worse due to missed payments, fines, and hefty legal expenses. If they can't keep up with their normal monthly payments, they won't be able to pay all of the extra fees, which might more than triple their late debt.

Owners facing foreclosure have 60 to 90 days from the day the notice of default (NOD) was issued to provide alternatives. Since the majority of owners really feel their financial issues are just temporary, it's essential to keep in mind that the owner's credit history is a significant component of your offer: If you can promptly purchase the house at a fair price, cure the default, or pay the past-due mortgage, the seller will avoid having the late payments appear on his credit record in place of a foreclosure (or possibly a bankruptcy, which is often the only alternative for owners who are unwilling to voluntarily resolve their cash flow problems). Long acknowledged as a significant driver for homeowners who are behind on their mortgage payments, the desire to maintain credit. Due to legislative initiatives to pardon defaults, the dynamics were significantly altered in 2008, and many homeowners are now just leaving their properties without worrying that their credit would prevent them from ever acquiring a property again.

To make sure the owner has equity in the property, find out the loan balance and the worth of the property before continuing. One reason having as much equity as possible is sometimes seen as helpful is the capacity to provide the owner some immediate cash to cover the expenses of leaving the home and finding a new place to live while you are selling. After deducting the whole cost of the purchase as well as the price of any repairs or modifications necessary to increase the property's resale value, the remaining equity in the property is what enables you to make a profit.

Some real estate experts advise paying the defaulting owner a small sum of money and then starting to pay off the existing debts right away because the lender might not allow you to simply step into the shoes of the original borrower, and the debt might be deemed in default. In other words, buy the property subject to the present liabilities. Check with your legal counsel to see whether the loan agreements have an assumption provision that would let you to lawfully absorb the debt. This process often involves submitting a loan application and paying a charge. Beware of terms that demand rapid payment upon the transfer of the property to a new owner and accelerate the whole loan. You must be on the lookout for this. If you discuss the hazards of your intended contract with a defaulting buyer with your legal counsel, they may be able to inform you of them.

Many issues that arise when purchasing foreclosures may be avoided by arranging the purchase agreement such that the owner is obligated to vacate the property as soon as is practically possible. Losing ownership is tough for a homeowner, but recognizing that she is no longer the owner while still living in the property may be even harder.

A sale happens as a result of a foreclosure.

The main distinction is whether the debt is protected by a deed of trust or a mortgage, in which case nonjudicial foreclosure is necessary and judicial foreclosure is essential.

A court enforced foreclosure.

A court-ordered foreclosure occurs when a lender sues a borrower to seize the property. Like with any other case, it starts with the court system delivering a summons and complaint on the borrower (along with any other parties with junior liens or encumbrances against the property). The lender has the power to foreclose if the borrower has shown a real problem (in which case alternate payment arrangements would be negotiated).

A default judgment is obtained when a borrower refuses to comply with a demand for payment. The lender may then request that a receiver be appointed by the court to execute the judgment. The lender then promotes the sale for a further four to six weeks before holding a public auction on the steps of the courthouse or town/city hall. The property will be repossessed if the lender does not get full payment. Although it might take as little as 3 months or as long as 12 months, depending on the circumstance, the whole court foreclosure procedure lasts, on average, 4 to 6 months.

A property may be foreclosed without a court order.

Lenders may use the power of sale clauses in the deed of trust to foreclose without going to court in countries that authorize nonjudicial foreclosure. The deed of trust identifies the trustee, who is in responsibility of preserving title for the length of the loan, the beneficiary (lender), and the grantor (borrower). A Notice of Default and a Notice of Sale are published in a legal publication if the borrower doesn't make the payments that they've agreed to.
If the loan is not fully restored before the trustee's sale date and time, a public auction or sheriff's sale, similar to a judicial foreclosure, will be held on the steps of a large public venue in town, such as a courthouse. If no one submits a bid, the asset is delivered to the lender, who provides the loan amount plus any fees and penalties. The property is transferred to the lender if no one makes a bid. This is the most frequent scenario, unless the property is valued and has equity, in which case a large number of interested bidders may participate in a free-for-all auction type auction.
If you do your research and are well knowledgeable about a property before making an offer, bidding on and purchasing homes at a foreclosure auction may be thrilling and even rewarding. A string of home runs may often make up for a single mistake in judgment, but being overconfident or depending too much on your gut emotions might be dangerous. Whatever the cause, it might be as simple as an unpaid tax payment or hidden physical issues like a cracked slab or rising dirt that cause your lemonade to change into a lemonade jar. Make that you have title insurance coverage and a seller-provided clean title report.

The time window for salvation is limited.

In certain countries, a borrower has the option to pay the whole amount owing, which includes the loan principal, late fees, the lender's legal charges, and all foreclosure sale costs, in order to retrieve her property at a foreclosure auction. The borrower is then able to regain possession of the property. The duration of the redemption period varies per state.
Additionally, this is a perfect time to go through the terms of the borrower's deed with them, if there is one. If the transaction is successful, the buyer will be given the right and the ability to redeem from the borrower.
Regardless of whether you prevail at the foreclosure auction, you are still required to provide the borrower a reasonable chance to regain the property throughout the state-mandated redemption period. Always keep in mind that you shouldn't make substantial alterations only to persuade the borrower to redeem the property so that you can then claim credit for transforming his troubled home into a lovely one.
Additionally, the bulk of the houses available for sale at a foreclosure auction are bought by lenders. Because the neighborhood building inspector or code enforcement office will be aware that a wealthy lender has acquired title to the property and will anticipate that all citations for poor conditions or code violations will be immediately corrected, deferred maintenance or code violations on the property may also result in a better deal. You may be able to relieve the lender of this obligation while also acquiring the power to negotiate a better bargain for yourself.

REO.

Given that foreclosed homes often change ownership among their lenders, your next chance to purchase the property may be via the real estate owned (REO) division of the lender, which specializes in the purchase of foreclosed properties. Some investors have concluded that because they won't have to deal with a troubled or dishonest seller, this is a great opportunity to purchase a home. Knowing the ins and outs of the lending institution's policies and practices for selling foreclosed homes might help you save money on real estate. The Resolution Trust Corporation no longer offers any premium real estate owned (REO) assets (RTC). The RTC was founded by Congress in the early 1990s as a quasi-federal government organization to dispose of the massive amount of foreclosed assets that the major lending banks had accumulated as a result of the real estate market decline. A once-in-a-lifetime opportunity for real estate investment emerged as a result of the large number of properties available, the RTC's relative inexperience, and the insufficient due diligence in certain areas of the nation. Smart real estate investors who had a lot of cash on hand, the rapid decision-making skills, and the resources to weather the market slump grasped this chance. Lenders are neither ignorant nor nice, yet late-night educational gurus continue to promote the usage of lender-owned properties (REOs). Even while nonperforming loans are a liability on a bank's balance sheet, it might be difficult for banks to sell a property for less than its market worth in order to completely erase it from their books.

The disposition experts in the REO department are seasoned professionals with in-depth knowledge of the regional housing markets and regular relationships to the top real estate agents in the region. Since they are often paid as a percentage of the selling price, these real estate brokers have an incentive to get the greatest possible price for their clients.

Since the lender did not spend the time and money necessary to physically repair and reposition the property to perform better in the market, a real estate investor with a REO only benefits from financing and the continuous operational losses that often arise.

Even when lenders have a large number of REOs, the Office of Thrift Supervision (OTS), a federal body that regulates many savings banks and savings-and-loan institutions and frequently audits their loan and REO portfolios, often puts limits on them.

Short sales might help you avoid both the REO and foreclosure procedures.

The greatest properties are those that are not offered on the open market, where price increases due to competition are possible. Astute real estate investors are aware of this. These homeowners have no equity in their houses, and the current amount of their debt is much more than the value of the loan. They are aware that sellers who are driven to sell will give the greatest prices, and there is no greater incentive for a homeowner to sell than the fear of facing foreclosure and having their credit destroyed. Even if the property was sold, the owners would still owe the lender more money than the sale's earnings. This was accurate for an increasing number of homes during the late 2000s housing market collapse. "doing more with less." is the driving principle of the short sale. It is conceivable to buy a house from the owner and work out a settlement with the lender or lien holder in which the latter accepts a full payment for the house that is less than the remaining amount owed on the current loan.

Recognizing the benefits of the vendor.

Many homeowners learned that they had negative equity in their houses in the late 2000s, when subprime and zero-down loans were accessible coupled with a decrease in property prices. Since the revenues from selling their houses wouldn't have been enough to pay off the debt, they were unable to do so (a situation known as being upside down).

Given their precarious financial situations and lack of alternative options, it seemed doubtful that many of these property owners would be able or willing to continue making payments on the debt service associated with the flooded property. The best course of action for a homeowner in this situation is a short sale.

Although a short sale doesn't pay the existing owner or seller any money, it does provide them with a speedy way out of a challenging circumstance in order to maintain their credit score (because he will likely want to be a homeowner again someday). Since the real estate investor is undoubtedly seeking for an excellent tenant, who better to rent to than the present tenant, the current owner will also benefit. The present owner may continue to reside there even if he is no longer the property's legal owner to avoid having his life disrupted. By enabling you to stay in your existing dwelling, the social stigma associated with homelessness is somewhat reduced. Additionally, finding a renter as quickly as possible could make it easier for you to get financing for the property.

Short sales are compared with other types of real estate.

Real estate investors often discover the hard way that purchasing REO or repossessed houses may be difficult. Even though foreclosed properties are often advertised and available to all prospective purchasers, there is sometimes not enough time or information to do in-depth due diligence prior to the sale. Examining foreclosed homes should be done with caution as they may contain unpleasant surprises.

The finest foreclosure auction properties often pique the attention of extra (often knowledgeable) purchasers who are willing to pay more for the property than you are if they believe they will be able to negotiate a better deal later. A short sale often allows you to negotiate a sale closing date that gives you more time to get financing for the balance, but you are also required to have 10% of the purchase price in cash on hand and to secure a loan for the balance within 30 days. A short sale may also help you avoid the problems connected with a borrower redemption if the court decides to foreclose on your house. It may be challenging to get property information for REO properties since lenders or their representatives may be reticent to cooperate with requests for inspections or details on the condition of the property. Although REOs have a reputation for being sold by lenders at any price, the truth is that they often sell for near to full market value when reduced for their condition and the short timeframes in which lenders want them to be sold.

Finding pre-foreclosure properties—homes where the owner has fallen behind on her debt service payments—and striking a deal with her to purchase the property before it is lost and her credit is damaged are the keys to making money in real estate. Due to the widespread usage of highly leveraged financing, when borrowers obtained loans equal to (or even more than) the whole market value of the property at the time of purchase, these types of scenarios have become increasingly frequent. Some debtors had more overall debt than their property was worth, which resulted in foreclosure.

Finding and cultivating prospective short-term sales prospects.

The concept looks to be lot simpler to put into practice than it really is. The most difficult situations to locate properties in are those where the owner is behind on payments but the lender has not received a Notice of Default.

Typically, you'll get a list of suitable houses from real estate agents or perhaps the financing companies themselves. As an alternative, you might drive around the neighborhoods you're interested in and look for signs that read "bank owned" On the other hand, owner-occupied pre-foreclosure homes that are ideal for a short sale might not show any signals of problems. This is especially true now, when several lenders are being advised to show more tolerance to customers who are several months behind on their mortgage payments.

If you're seeking for these possibilities, you may find many resources online. Others try to reach agreements on alternate payment plans or loan modifications with both borrowers and lenders. Despite the fact that many of these efforts fail, they do provide information on property owners who could be eligible for a short sale in certain situations.

You may look for potential short sale properties after receiving a Notice of Default from your mortgage company. Since this document is out to the public, other real estate investors may get in touch with the owner to discuss a short sale.

This information is available during a standard foreclosure, and many purchasers would be willing to consider a short sale as an alternative to a traditional foreclosure during the pre-foreclosure stage. Of course, you also need to persuade the present owner and the loan provider.

In order to improve your prospects of selling the property, keep in mind that lien holders may have gotten a good deal on the underlying debt and may be open to negotiating a reduced payment with you. Your research will often show if a defaulted debt has recently been sold; this is important information that might help you create a winning negotiating approach.

When there are foreclosed homes in your region, short sales are often advised, but approach with caution: It is advised that the property be thoroughly evaluated. Actually, you need more opportunities and access to the land than you now have. As we've seen, while it's not as awful as foreclosures, short sale homes may also be properties that the owner is ready to walk away from for a variety of reasons. Approach carefully since what can seem like a once-in-a-lifetime opportunity might really lead to financial ruin.

Short sales are challenging for lenders to approve.

You can have trouble persuading your lender to agree to a short sale of your home or other property in addition to the difficulties of finding a short sale opportunity. Since the federal government has just recently begun requiring lenders to treat borrowers with unusual tolerance and cooperation, it is believed that this trend will persist. Some lenders may not be able to manage the huge amount of negative equity loans and requests to amend current credit agreements they receive. On the one hand, lenders are pushed to think about short sales, but they are also required to provide a plan for relieving the present loan default. Lenders will likely be less hesitant to cooperate with short sales as a result of this tendency. Lenders' business plans and financial goals impact a short sale's long-term viability. The lenders are fully aware that payments aren't being paid, and it's practically a given that they'll finish the foreclosure process, keep the house for a while, and incur expenditures before trying to sell it.

Other options to renting

You may continue to own a home with a lease option and ultimately purchase it without having to put down a significant down payment. A lease option is essentially simply two contracts combined. In this case, there is a lease (rental agreement) in place with all the usual limitations, but the renter also has the only right to purchase the property in the future if certain requirements are completed.

The owner must sell the property if the lease option is used, but the renter is not obligated to purchase it. Bilateral agreements between parties are unilateral until the tenant uses his right of choice. One of the most important considerations when it comes to leasing options is the option price (buying price) that the buyer is required to pay. It is more common for this amount to be an anticipated future value based on expected growth and the window of opportunity for exercising the option to purchase the shares. This amount may be a fixed price based on the stock's current market value. In a market where the seller anticipates a 5% yearly gain, a property worth $200,000 today may be offered as a lease option with a $210,000 option price that can be exercised at any time over the course of the following 12 months. Naturally, if the option price exceeds the property's market worth, a wise buyer won't exercise the option.

Finding lease choices is considerably simpler when there are few bids and owners are motivated to sell, and a better price may be negotiated. The most common real estate types for which lease options are employed are single-family houses and condominiums, while the concept may be used to any kind of property. No matter where you are in the nation, there is almost always more demand than supply for leasing opportunities.

Please remember that for many first-time home purchasers, leasing alternatives are a terrific way to ease into the process. They aren't only for speculators in real estate. Since there is a huge discrepancy between the demand for leasing choices and the availability of them, you may need to place your own ad in order to find lease opportunities. Another technique to locate a good rental choice is to respond to "properties for rent" advertisements. A little advertising might generate a lot of interest when you own a property and want to lease it out.

Reviewing the results of auctions and probate sales

It is essential to bring up probate or estate sales when discussing some of the most unique real estate deals. Additionally, as the number of people using the Internet rises, auctions are becoming a common method to sell real estate.

Sales happen all through the probate procedure.

Mortality, which is even more certain than taxes, makes it feasible to buy high-quality real estate at reasonable costs. Every day, someone in your neighborhood passes away, leaving real estate in the hands of their heirs, who may or may not decide to keep it up. Since there may be delays or even a need for court permission before the sale can go through, it is important to get familiar with the rules and regulations in your area that regulate probate transactions. Under the guidance of probate attorneys, the estate's executors sell these properties during probate sales (or by the public administrator if the owner dies without a trust or will). Furthermore, in these auctions, overbidding is often seen. The overbid strategy may be used by interested bidders to outbid you and buy the property for a higher price than the current offer being taken into consideration (prior to the court issuing an order approving the probate sale). In order to overbid, your bid typically has to be at least 5% higher than the one being accepted. Recognize the opportunity and be prepared to adjust your offer if necessary. But try to avoid being drawn into a bidding conflict and overpaying for a home. Before you begin bidding, choose your own limit price.

A real estate auction is held.

Builders and investors think one of the most popular methods for showing their surplus inventory of homes in various places is to host real estate auctions, in which businesses claim to be selling good real estate at below-market costs. Contrary to popular belief, foreclosure sales—which are often called auctions—should not be confused with these auctions. We're talking about open auctions, when antiques and artifacts could be put up for sale alongside other things on the same day. Even new home builders have turned to private auctions to sell their new homes in hot real estate markets in order to generate interest and excitement in areas where there is a shortage of demand for new homes.

This technique of selling property to the public is used by private parties, governmental entities, and real estate auction firms. Real estate auctioneers are often included in the yellow pages of your local phone book. This auction's objective, like all others, is to increase the selling price by fostering competition and interest among prospective purchasers. A minimum or reserve price is often established to prevent the seller from selling the house for too little money.

These real estate auctions are frequently publicized in newspapers, radio and television stations, and online, with example prices that appeal to prospective buyers. They advertise a wide variety of homes, but often include a few that seem unreal, like 10 acres of spotless property for $5,000. The property is in a rural place, thus it stands to reason that no one is aware of its precise location.

We believe that since there are so many bidders competing for the same exclusive, expensive property, auctions seldom provide investors great investment opportunities. Furthermore, since the reserve price or minimum price is so near to the property's true market worth, the buyer is essentially paying full retail while believing she is receiving a great bargain. To see whether there is anything interesting being offered, look out these auctions since excellent possibilities do sometimes present themselves.

Research an auction property as thoroughly as you would a foreclosed or REO property. Due to the limited time before the auction or the auctioneer's incapacity to provide the essential information, thorough due diligence is often not feasible. Hiring a reputable business to do a Phase I environmental review, for instance, is the most effective way to reduce the likelihood that the property may have some expensive environmental concerns that will need to be handled.

You won't be able to buy one for each property you want to bid on during an auction. Do your homework before making a choice since doing so might lead to a number of risks when purchasing real estate. Real estate is one asset from which you cannot back out if you make a mistake. Remember that you want to avoid any unpleasant shocks!

If you place the highest offer and win the auction, you must immediately provide the seller a certified money check for at least 10% of the winning amount. Your actual closing date will most likely occur during the next thirty days. Real estate auctions are most often advertised online. Similar to many other online possibilities, you must take great care to confirm that the company you are dealing with is reputable before continuing. No matter how good a bargain may seem, never purchase real estate without first seeing it.

Chapter Four

Investment Types/Strategies

Wholesaling is the strategy that newcomers to real estate investing use the most often. It has the ability to make money quickly since it requires little resources, commitments, or obligations. Flipping is the practice of persuading a seller to accept a low price or favourable terms in exchange for reselling the agreement to a new buyer for a greater price or commission.

Even when the retail worth of their house is $275,000 or more, a homeowner will often agree to sell it for $200,000 nevertheless. Once a contract is signed, the wholesaler locates a client willing to pay more than $200,000, such as $210,000 or $215,000. At the conclusion of the contract, the wholesaler receives a $10,000–$15,000 spread.

Wholesalers should purchase real estate for 65% of the true market worth, or even less is better, and then sell it to investors for around 70% of that price. Real estate owners must be willing to sell their property for at least 65% of what it is now worth, and real estate investment purchasers must be ready to pay at least 70% of the property's market value, both of which must occur for this to happen. Real estate owners who are willing to offer their houses for less than 65% of their value make up a very small percentage of sellers. And when you go to areas with more costly houses, nicer residences, and freshly built real estate, the numbers become less and smaller. However, as you go closer to the older, less affluent, and less clean portions of town, the number of possible wholesale discounts explodes. Why?

First off, most recently built homes do not have enough equity for a wholesaler to purchase a property for 65 cents on the dollar since most of them have liens on the land roughly equal to their worth.

Second, when real estate prices increase, it becomes more difficult to maintain the same percentages. 65 percent of $100,000, for instance, is $65,000, and 65 percent of $1,000,000, $650,000. Maintaining such favorable percentages becomes increasingly challenging as the price climbs.

Third, finding buyers isn't nearly as difficult, despite the condition of the house, since the nicer parts of town are more in demand. Most homeowners in desirable areas may simply list their property on the Multiple Listing Service (MLS) with a neighborhood real estate agent, and if priced well, it will sell quickly.

Fourth, more expensive houses are easier to sell, and the majority of owners of well-maintained properties are unwilling to accept such a low asking price.

Fifth, on average, homeowners in more affluent and prestigious neighborhoods have the means, know-how, and assets to effectively sell a house such that it brings in more than 65% of its value. Since property owners can now quickly get an online appraisal of their property's worth with a few keystrokes, unlike in the past, it is more harder for wholesalers to find deals at 65 cents on the dollar or less. As a consequence, older, less wealthy, and/or rougher parts of town are where you'll find wholesale discounts more often, and if a property is in poorer shape, the owner will be more willing to haggle a lower price for it.

Wholesaling raises an ethical issue that is seldom ever acknowledged or addressed. Wholesalers may only put a property under contract for 65 percent of fair value or less where the owner is uninformed of other choices or has an inaccurate perception of the property's real value. Are you truly aiding a seller if you persuade them to accept a price of 65 percent or less when you're aware that they have no concept what they're dealing with? This ethical dilemma may arise throughout your investing career. Most property owners can get in touch with a real estate agent by giving them a quick call, and if that agent takes the time to market the home on the MLS successfully, most sellers should expect to get at least 80% of the asking price. In other instances, the open market price increased to as much as 90%.

Some investors think a deal has been made "if the seller is delighted with what I've supplied." Others believe that "if I know this seller could simply list this property on the MLS and make $25,000 more than selling it to me for 65 cents on the dollar, then I need to at least share this information with the seller so that they can make a more informed decision" and "if I know this seller could simply list this property on the MLS and make $25,000 more than selling it to me for 65 cents on the dollar." then I need to at least share this information with the seller so that they can make a more informed decision.

Both parties may have concerns to discuss apart from ethical ones. The seller may start to second-guess their choice after the contract has been signed if they are not aware of all options, such as placing the property on the MLS with an agent. Even before you close, the owner can be aware that they are only getting a fraction of what their house is really worth. The next thing they'll do is utilize all available legal options to end their contract with you (legal or otherwise). As you learned in the lesson on pleasure and pain, when someone feels taken advantage of, they will go to any lengths to put things right.

If you show a seller how they can get far more for their sale than you are ready to provide, you run the risk of losing the deal entirely. Proponents of educating property owners about their options claim that some owners may find the knowledge valuable and choose to cooperate with you to avoid further conflicts with real estate agents or other visitors. It's more probable that the seller will not back out of the agreement before it closes if they decide to sell to you despite your lesser offer, keeping everyone happy. In such cases, you may be certain that you provided the vendor with a range of options. Before allowing property owners to choose which option is best for them, we strongly suggest our students to offer all of their options to them.

Everything, including single-family homes and large shopping centers, is offered at wholesale prices. However, certain assets provide wonderful niche markets for the traditional wholesale strategy. The wholesale of empty lots is a thriving business.

Land for development is often sought after by local developers. Due to the asset's simplicity and lack of complexity, vacant lots are among the fastest and simplest conventional wholesales to accomplish (zoning and whether or not it has electricity, water, or sewage running to it). Furthermore, because the majority of people don't live in vacant houses, the person you want to sell to will have problems getting in touch with the owner. When a new customer contacts the original seller directly rather than going via the wholesaler, wholesalers get quite anxious.

Another fantastic wholesale market is older abandoned houses in areas where many new luxury residences are being constructed and demolished. A land may be bought for $200,000, the existing building torn down, and two million dollar luxury castles built there. Selling wholesale from an empty house is significantly easier.

Older houses in a neighborhood that has just undergone renovations make up another attractive wholesale sector. If you want to find these places, look for dumpsters in the driveways of abandoned houses nearby. This suggests that real estate speculators have moved into the area and are buying older properties to rebuild into more modern residences that command far greater prices than the neighborhood did.

In this line of work, it helps to anticipate where the next crucial location will be so you can go there first. As you can see, traditional wholesaling works well in certain situations. The objective of traditional wholesaling, after all, is to complete a deal as soon as possible, place it under contract, and then sell the goods. If everything works well, these agreements might be quite lucrative and bring in a lot of money quickly.

Wholesalers and retailers.

The phrase "retail wholesale," coined by our team, describes the practice of offering a property at a discount to a retail consumer. Typically, the property is sold to a separate investor in a wholesale deal. In certain cases, this is the most cost-effective option. Usually, when a property is vacant land, as in the case above, or when a property is in such bad shape that it requires much more than just cosmetic maintenance.

Our team discovered that selling a transaction to a retail customer as opposed to an investor might often provide a 10x return on the same amount of work. The fact that some retail buyers aren't picky and are prepared to make concessions on issues with property quality shocks the majority of people. In fact, many people who buy homes on the open market want to paint them and make other little cosmetic modifications. Additionally, some motivated sellers have homes in high or exceptional condition. The result was the creation of the retail wholesale approach, which involves flipping a property in the same way as a traditional wholesale but selling it to a consumer (a retail buyer) rather than an investment buyer in order to make much bigger profits.

Another advantage of having this investing strategy in your toolkit is the possibility that certain transactions may not have enough equity to be lucrative as a traditional wholesale but may have enough equity as a retail wholesale. Consider the following illustration: On a home that is worth $400,000, the borrower owes $350,000.

Even if there is a lot of equity, an investment buyer cannot afford to pay cash for a house and still make money for a wholesaler. Do you remember the 65 percent rule? $40000 divided by 65% results in $260,000. Retail wholesale may be the best choice in this situation. The plan is to sign a contract to buy the property for a certain amount with the intention of selling it to another buyer for a higher price later on.

Instead of transferring the contract to the new client, a retail wholesaler would often carry out two separate closings, commonly referred to as contemporaneous or back-to-back closings.

Both traditional wholesale and retail wholesale transactions are investments made without the use of cash or credit. The bulk of investment opportunities that seem to be credit- and cash-free really involve untapped markets that want cash. When the contract with the seller is finished, you could just be able to put down a single dollar as earnest money and you might not have any other out-of-pocket expenses. You may still make a lot of money buying and selling real estate without any money or credit.

Retail wholesale may be up to 10 times more expensive than standard wholesale. When compared to selling to an investor, who could only pay you $3,000, selling to a retail consumer might get you $30,000 or more. But as the economy expands, so does the need for a transaction that is far more involved and possibly challenging. This is mostly because traditional mortgage loans, some of which may have extremely rigorous underwriting standards, are often used by retail buyers to buy real estate. In addition to stopping illegal flipping in its tracks, some underwriting requirements put in place to counter it have also made it difficult for legal flipping to occur. You'll learn later on that executing a retail wholesale successfully depends on having the right mortgage expert on your team.

Options.

Both traditional and retail wholesaling are similar to real estate optioning. You are asking the chance to buy someone else's property when you ask for an option. This resembles the purchase contract you may sign with a homeowner to buy their home.

The primary distinction between an option and a conventional purchase contract is that an option often lasts for a number of years, which is substantially longer than a standard purchase contract (usually 30 to 60 days). In a manner similar to a wholesale transaction, the option investor may then choose to buy the asset and hold onto it, sell it to a different bidder, or do all three.

Since corporate transactions take significantly longer to complete than house acquisitions, options are often used in them.

Chapter Five

How to Manage Your Property

Depending on the situation, a property manager may be in charge of every aspect of managing a building, including marketing, tenant selection, rent collecting, maintenance, and accounting. Many first-time real estate investors handle all aspects of management themselves, including rent collection, bill payment, showing rental homes to prospective tenants, painting, cleaning, and maintenance. On the other side, the vast majority of investors ultimately assign responsibilities they dislike or are inadequate for. It seems to reason that some inexperienced landlords are successful in running their rental properties on their own timetable. Others, though, have learned via on-the-job property management training how expensive errors may occur.

Taking stock of your existing circumstance and thinking through your self-management possibilities.

You may wish to consider managing your own property if you have the necessary abilities, the necessary time, and you reside close to your property. The following benefits of self-management are listed:

By avoiding recurring fees for property management, you save money.

Given the high cost of property management services, you may be able to save a lot of money by managing the property yourself. However, as we'll see in a minute, you should think about the overall worth of your time and estimate how much of it is spent on property upkeep.

Costs associated with maintenance may be decreased.

By maintaining direct control over management, you may choose the person who will be in charge of doing repairs and mowing the grass. Doing your own maintenance and yard work is often a smart option if you have the skills and time to do it. Hiring someone else to do it for you might quickly deplete your monthly cash flow, particularly in the first few years of ownership when cash flow is frequently limited. Make a list of trustworthy landscapers and handymen with legal permits and reasonable rates.

Investors in real estate often underestimate the amount of time they spend on management problems. Many self-managing landlords wouldn't be able to put a number on how much money they "saved" by forgoing a property manager's services.

If you make a livelihood doing anything other than managing rental properties, keeping up with your investment property may not be the best use of your time.

As a full-time, higher-earning professional, taking time off during the workweek to address a small problem at your rental property is not only impractical, but it might also be detrimental to your job and opportunities in the future.

Estimate your hourly rate for those of you who are employed based on your earnings from the prior year. Calculate the amount of money you'll save by buying and managing your house on your own. It is often better to engage a property manager for your rental properties unless doing so results in considerable financial savings compared to your current work.

You must follow the same rules and regulations whether you are a single owner or self-employed. Working hours may be more flexible than in a typical 9 to 5 employment. However, if you only have the opportunity to save $25 per hour and earn $50 per hour, it doesn't make sense to spend hours of your valuable workday handling rental properties.

Identifying and evaluating your own interests and talents.

To be given consideration for the position, you must hold the relevant qualifications. To get started, you don't need a degree or a lot of experience, and it's almost a guarantee that you'll think up some fresh ideas for how to make things better as you go.

The following questions about your personality and abilities might help you decide whether you are ready to be your own property manager:

Do you love interacting with people? The owner's work as a landlord is labor of love. Despite the fact that others often undervalue you, you must like connecting with people and solving issues.

- Do you have the strength of character to overcome obstacles? The ability to politely and rationally respond to complaints and service requests is crucial.
- Do you understand the foundations of accounting and how to use a calculator? Do you likewise treat your documents with the utmost care?
- Do you have any experience with effectively maintaining things? Working with your hands is beneficial, but if you can also recruit and manage seasoned contractors, you will have an advantage.
- It's crucial to be accessible to work on the weekends, late into the evenings, and to answer calls. Isn't it true that weekends are a waste of time?
- Do you have strong negotiating and sales skills? You will need to find a buyer for the property.
- Are you willing to put in the necessary time and effort? Other key duties that take a lot longer include selecting a fair rental rate and understanding property management legislation.

Avoid working as a property manager if you are easily influenced or become irritated at work. The way you communicate with your renters should always be professional. They must have the impression that you are someone who is willing to take responsibility for both the condition of the building and the efficiency of the unit. You must also ensure that tenants uphold the conditions of the lease, such as prompt rent payment and no property damage. The rental property management must deal firmly, equitably, and cordially with all rental professionals and tenants that engage with the property. You must maintain your composure, patience, and fairness when under pressure. When it comes to collecting rent and keeping your rules and standards, you must be resolute and unbending. You should also have a positive outlook while in treatment. Is it truly as easy as it seems to be?

When you manage a rental property, your responsibilities go beyond merely taking care of your present renters. As a landlord, you must also make contact with potential tenants, clients, suppliers, workers, neighbors, and officials. People, not physical property, are often at blame for rental management issues. Expect to be adaptable and to gain knowledge from your rental property management experiences. In addition to degrees, great real estate managers have learned their trade via trial and error. Practice makes perfect, as the saying goes.

Professional management firms pledge to hire competent staff members and assume full responsibility for the building's daily operations. The correct property manager may substantially influence the amount of cash flow generated by your rental property by quickly finding suitable substitute tenants and making sure that maintenance is completed on time and within budget. You need a property manager who is dedicated to helping you increase the value of your rental properties. Choose a property manager who has experience managing investments like yours. After completing some study, you should be able to choose the one that is most suitable for your home.

A poor management business may eat into your revenues and ultimately make your home unprofitable by charging expensive fees, providing poor upkeep, and renting to low-quality tenants. The results of selecting a poor property management firm may be substantially worse than if you managed the property yourself.

When you visit the offices of your property management firm, take the time to speak with the specific property manager who will be in charge of overseeing your rental property personally. Make a few more phone calls to references to confirm them, and don't sign a management contract unless you are convinced the organization you are hiring has a good track record. Simply checking the advice of the property management firm is insufficient. Utilize the list of all of their customers to get in touch with owners of rental properties that are the same size and kind as yours. Check to see whether the landlords you talk to have enough experience working with the property management firm to give you a trustworthy assessment.

Whether you're shopping for management for a single-family home, condominium, or small rental property, be sure the business you hire specializes in real estate. Many real estate sales offices (as opposed to property management corporations) provide property management services; however, these offices often focus on acquiring the listing in order to sell the property later. In contrast to property managers employed by property management firms, many property managers in real estate sales offices lack the qualifications, experience, and knowledge of a staff member of a property management company. The skills needed to manage real estate assets vary greatly from those needed to represent consumers.

Take into account the following issues as well:

Licenses.

Property managers often require both a real estate license and a property manager's license in order to do business. On the phone or online, confirm that the management company's and property manager's licenses are valid and current.

Credentials.

Verify the qualifications of the property management firm as well. The Institute of Real Estate Management (IREM), a group of licensed property managers, offers professional certifications including Certified Property Manager (CPM) and Accredited Residential Manager (ARM). Only a very small fraction of management companies are given the title of Accredited Management Organization (AMO). Visit www.irem.org to see whether your manager has Institute of Risk Management approval.

Insurance.

The company should keep professional liability insurance, general liability insurance, car liability insurance, and worker's compensation insurance (errors and omissions). Since they will act as your agent and collect your rent and security deposits, the management business should get a sizable fidelity bond. If an employee embezzles or inappropriately utilizes your money, you will be protected.

Accounting.

Look for a property management business that keeps a distinct accounting system for each property handled rather than a master trust account where money from several customers is combined.

Pertaining to money.

Property management firms often have the latitude and authority to conduct urgent repairs without the owner's permission under most management agreements. Naturally, this architecture allows the property management sector to respond quickly to unanticipated problems. According to the National Association of Realtors, the majority of management contracts provide property managers the authority to make repairs up to a certain monetary number without the owner's permission. The restriction must be suitable for the nature and dimensions of the property. A little duplex could only be subject to a $250 restriction, but commercial structures and bigger houses would be limited to $2,500.

Keep a close eye on the charges related to your new management company in the early stages of your partnership. Even if they may be permitted to utilize money somewhat lawfully, they nonetheless need to keep you continually updated on their activities. Maintaining these staff members occupied with repairs at the properties they supervise may be a profitable profit center for the maintenance teams that many management firms employ. Low administrative costs may be offered with the hope that higher maintenance fees would make up for it (often unnecessary). Choose a property management company that does not charge extra for upkeep, supplies, or materials.

Management companies often get a portion of the gross rental revenue in exchange for managing a property. For the whole property they manage, some management firms levy a flat monthly fee or charge a certain amount per unit. Try to work with a firm whose management charge is based on a percentage of sales; such a fee gives the management company a strong incentive to get and maintain market rents. As the size of the rental property grows, the percentage of the management charge reduces.

Typical management costs for single-family houses, condominiums, and small rental properties range from 9 to 10%; for medium-sized buildings, they range from 6 to 8%; and for massive residential complexes with 200 units or more, they range from 3 to 5%. The residential fee plan and the commercial fee schedule are identical.

Since tenant turnover takes up the majority of property management work, higher rents for vacant space are often acceptable. The property manager is in charge of screening possible tenants when a tenant vacates and preparing a rental apartment, commercial, industrial, or retail space for showings. Residential rental fees are often either a one-time payment of a few hundred dollars or a percentage of the rent, such as half of the monthly rental rate, depending on the situation. For leases of commercial, industrial, or retail property, the commission is often a percentage of the gross rent, with the amount decreasing as the lease period lengthens. As the lease period becomes longer, the percentage decreases.

Looking around for any potential environmental issues

Make sure your rental homes are a safe and healthy environment by following these measures. Despite the financial and legal ramifications of not making the disclosures needed by state and federal regulations, the majority of landlords simply do not want their tenants to get ill or injured in the first place. Think about the following issues:

Lead.

There can still be lead paint in some older buildings (which was banned in 1978). A lead test is the only way to determine if there is lead present. Since lead removal methods may discharge significant quantities of lead dust into the environment, controlling the lead is often preferable than removing it. As a property owner, you should be aware of the dangers presented by lead as well as the particular disclosures required by law for residential rental units. To eliminate lead dangers, almost every state has approved laws, some of which also include testing and maintenance requirements in addition to the federal disclosure requirements.

Asbestos.

Despite the fact that there are no federal requirements for asbestos disclosure in rental homes and no federal duties to investigate or remove asbestos, local and state authorities should be contacted to determine whether any disconnection requirements exist. The usage of asbestos improved the strength, heat insulation, and fire resistance of many products. Most of the goods have been bonded to prevent asbestos from leaking into the environment. Since no fibers are evacuated during this process, there are no recognized health hazards. If disturbed, asbestos may be very deadly. A considerable number of asbestos fibers inhaled raises the risk of getting lung and other types of cancer, according to research on people who have been exposed to asbestos. You shouldn't do your own asbestos testing. Use the services of an experienced environmental testing company since it might be dangerous to disassemble possibly asbestos-containing artifacts to get samples because asbestos could be dispersed into the air.

Radon is a radioactive gas that causes cancer and is both invisible and odorless. It may be found in the rocks and soil of every region of the United States. High radon gas concentrations have been linked to the development of lung cancer in certain structures. On the other hand, since concentrations are often below permissible levels, the majority of the radon in buildings poses no immediate danger. Although radon disclosure and testing are not legally required, more people are becoming aware of this potentially dangerous problem. Test for radon at your rental properties using easy, low-cost methods, and then consult with local authorities to learn more about its presence and the best course of action.

Due to the purported health hazards, mold spore exposure has been the subject of much controversy recently. Mold has been around since and may be found in practically every environment. However, as seen by a number of high-profile cases brought in recent years, assertions that certain forms of mold may be fatal have only lately been raised. At the start of the 1990s, the city of New York developed standards and a process for mold treatment, but the Environmental Protection Agency didn't provide any data until March 2001. The EPA standards often adhere to the New York City method, which entails a number of specific steps depending on the size of the mold-infested space. Despite the fact that some people have complained of respiratory illnesses after being exposed to high mold levels, there are currently no scientific standards in place to determine what exposure levels are appropriate. However, landlords must take allegations of mold exposure carefully. You may lessen the possibility that mold will grow in your building by identifying and eliminating moisture infiltration as soon as it occurs. You must follow the EPA's regulations if your renter alleges that mold is developing in the structure. If the issue is serious and persistent, you should seek expert help. To lessen the likelihood that you may be subject to legal action from your renters, use certified specialists and meticulously record all talks.

Chapter Six

Bargaining Strategies

Since the market often overestimates the worth of the item being sold, you may always lower the asking price in a sluggish market. If at all possible, you should provide financial aid to the vendor in order to get the greatest price. Find out how much similar homes have sold for in the past to be prepared by doing some research.

Recognize the variables that influenced the seller's decision to sell. For instance, selling real estate could be necessary as a consequence of a divorce, a relocation, or a loss of employment. Even if a seller's emotional drive may come from retirement or a death in the family, each of these events has a unique effect on the seller's emotional motivation and desire to sell. The seller, for instance, may have purchased a new house and wanted to sell the old one in order to get financing for the new one. For example, if the seller is a landlord, he may be exhausted from managing tenants and caring for the property. Alternatively, he could require the money from the sale of the house since he's bankrupt as a result of a financial overstretch. You'll be able to negotiate with the owner more effectively if you comprehend the reasons behind the owner's desire to sell.

Great offers may sometimes be discovered, both in terms of price and service requirements. The greatest bids are often available in a buyer's market when a seller needs to sell right now. An offer that is below market value will either be accepted or rejected depending on the circumstances. If you're unhappy with how a business connection has developed, don't be afraid to end it. Despite what the seller would have you think, there's a chance that if your offer is accepted, it won't be the only one on the table at this moment. In order to prevent having to repeat the bargaining process, you should cease walking away as soon as a seller becomes motivated. As a result, you'll have a better chance of getting additional discounts. Transactions are not interchangeable.

A kind of loan where the seller contributes to the cost of purchasing the property is known as seller financing.

Everyone wins in this situation if the presentation is done effectively. Lenders are customers who get financing from a vendor for their purchases (also known as seller-financed loans or purchase-money loans). Hard money lenders are less willing than sellers to accept a lower interest rate from borrowers. The seller could be ready to carry a loan at a rate of 6 percent in exchange for payment of 3 percent in a savings account, even if the current mortgage rate is 7 percent. This is particularly helpful for investors with a little down payment as motivated sellers are more likely to accept a first or second offer. Here's how to go about it:

- If the owner agrees to finance the sale, offer to pay nothing for the first six months. This gives you a backup plan in case you later decide to modify or sell the house with the goal of renting it out. The owner-financed loan could be repaid in full using the rental revenue. The worst-case scenario in this circumstance is that nothing takes place at all.
- Make careful to pay down the minimum amount of money possible so that you may keep the money you need for repairs. This approach to negotiating a home renovation might be quite effective. Despite the fact that some investors have asked for no money to be put down, I believe that making a little deposit is a good faith gesture that would be welcomed.

- Ask for a loan with the longest duration available and an interest rate below the going rate (30 years or more).
- Ask for the rent to be included in the price when buying a rental property. You will thus be qualified for credit for the two to three months after the transfer of the property to you. The vendor will thus be in responsible of collecting payments, and you will get three months' rent as compensation.
- Make it a condition that every piece of furniture, such as the carpet, window coverings, air conditioners, and appliances, must stay with the home.
- Tell the seller that, if at all possible, you would want to finalize the deal right away. If you want to sell and resell your home, a longer closing term will offer you more time to locate a new buyer.
- Before you sign the contract, insist that the seller covers all closing fees, including title insurance.

Since every dollar the buyer saves is a dollar the seller saves, always offer the lowest price. Ask the seller to cover any necessary repairs or provide you with a credit on the purchase price so you can afford to get these items fixed. To be on the safe side, make your price reasonable; stay away from charging an amount that would disgrace the provider.

If you decide not to complete the purchase, a weasel or contingency clause in your contract should provide you the legal right to withdraw. This clause should be included in every contract. The most typical contingency clauses include the following:

- To complete the deal, financing at (whatever percent is chosen) for 30 years (or whatever many years are needed) is required. Prior to closing, the buyer must personally view the property and provide their approval of its state.
- Before closing, the buyer's spouse, business partner, or any other parties involved must provide their approval.
- Prior to Closing, the Buyer's Contractor must examine the property and provide his approval.
- Before the sale may be finalized, the buyer must get an approved house inspection report.
- The buyer must review and accept the purchase agreement, leases, tenant histories, title work, and repair bids before the transaction is consummated.
- If a written contract has a 24- or 48-hour expiry date, the courts will rule it voidable. This gives the seller the option to reject your offer, and it prevents rival agents from publicizing your contract and enlisting the help of their friends to raise the asking price of your home.

Financing.

You need to know where to look for exceptional real estate possibilities and how to get the funds needed to execute these fantastic deals if you want to be a successful real estate investor.

There are many possible sources of funding. You may borrow money from a variety of sources, including banks, mortgage lenders, and private equity firms. In other circumstances, using alternate funding techniques, such as borrowing money from family, friends, or other investors seeking a decent return on their investment, may be necessary. Alternatively, you might refinance your present home and use the equity to invest in other real estate. For example, you may seek a bank loan or borrow money against the equity of your principal property. Although it's hazardous, using a credit card to buy real estate is nevertheless a possibility.

Taking out a loan to invest in real estate is dangerous, particularly if you're a beginner. All debts must be settled, particularly those owing to friends and family. Late payments may have a negative effect on your credit score. If you are unable to repay them in full, you could have to declare bankruptcy. If you want to keep a long-term connection with a private investor, paying them late might be just as detrimental.

By maintaining a financial reserve that you can utilize as a fallback in case anything goes wrong, you can prevent becoming bankrupt. Before moving on, be sure an investment will provide a profit.

Mortgages.

Before you may be approved for a mortgage, one of the three major credit reporting agencies will evaluate your credit and verify your income. A FICO credit score is created using data from a credit report. Most people consider anything with a credit score of 700 or above to be a good credit risk.

You will be required to provide documentation of your income, job, and any other passive sources of income if a lender has any concerns about your capacity to make payments or maintain an investment property. Your desire to rent out the property is known to the bank, but they will only credit you for each payment at a rate of 75%. The remaining 75% are available for other purposes, leaving 25% for vacancies, maintenance, taxes, and insurance. You could be eligible for an owner-occupied loan to aid with your home purchase. You must reside in a house for at least a year before opting to turn it into a rental. Consequently, the interest rate on your loan is cheaper.

Investigate the many mortgage choices that are now offered to you. While some of them will meet your needs, others won't.

Mortgage defense

The equity in your properties may be used to pay off your loan in full if you have a blanket mortgage that covers all of your properties (or more than one). If you're having trouble being accepted for a new loan but have other assets that might be used as security, you might be able to refinance your existing loan with a blanket mortgage. This has the disadvantage of tying up your cash and maybe jeopardizing your other real estate investments.

A mortgage that includes a range of benefits.

You may combine a new loan and an existing loan into one transaction with the aid of this tool. The most typical situation is "blending." It is the act of adding the interest rates from the two loans to determine the interest rate for the new loan. When two loans are arranged jointly rather than separately, the overall interest rate is often lower. Blended mortgages are a flexible financing option that may be used to many different situations. If the seller agrees, the buyer may be able to reduce the interest rate on the seller's current low-interest loan.

Mortgage payments are paid in installments.

A GMP first reduces payments before progressively raising them over a predetermined amount of time. After then, payroll payments begin to level out for the remainder of the load period. If you believe your income will increase over time, you must take advantage of this opportunity. Starting with a smaller monthly payment using this strategy also has the advantage of making it simpler to get authorized for a bigger loan. Negative amortization is a disadvantage of the configuration. You can wind up paying more than you would have if you had taken out a basic loan as opposed to refinancing your mortgage since the interest you save is added to your mortgage.

Mortgages with adjustable rates have decreasing payments over time.

The low starting payments are graded in years 2, 3, and 4 and the loan is accelerated in year 5, which is the sole difference between this and a GMP. (Payment by balloon).

A mortgage is given on a pledged account.

The buyer contributes a down payment of at least 10% of the purchase price to a pledged savings account.

Any loan with a variable or adjustable interest rate.

The interest rate, which is adjusted once a year to reflect changes in the market, determines how much is owed. If interest rates rise in the future, taking advantage of low interest rates today might place you in a bad financial situation. But I've just come to understand that interest rate changes have an impact on much more than simply interest rates. The amount of the monthly installments is also checked to make sure that the loan will be repaid within the specified 30-year time frame, neither sooner or later. If you can make a little monthly principle payment, the lender will reduce the amount of mortgage payments required to ensure that the loan is repaid within the 30-year period provided in the loan agreement.

To qualify for a 15- or 30-year repayment plan, both the borrower and the lender must agree that the mortgage would be periodically renegotiated or "rolled over" The lender will benefit if interest rates increase in this situation. Throughout the buying process, the buyer has the option to refinance at any moment.

The Federal Housing Administration and the Veterans Administration both provide mortgage guarantees.

Get in contact with your financial institution right away to find out whether you qualify for one of these loans with a little or no down payment. They are protected by the government.

Assumable mortgages are those that can be refinanced if the borrower is unable to make payments.

The process of obtaining nonqualifying assumable loans was simple back then. However, things are different now. You could still be eligible for assumable loans if you follow the guidelines established by the bank that provided the first loan. After your loan has been accepted, lenders are free to raise the interest rate. You are assuming a loan when you agree to pay the seller's installments out of the money the seller owes the bank. If you have extra money and want to take advantage of an interest rate that is lower than the typical variable rate, you may pick this option. Unless the seller agrees to seller-finance the equity gap, you will be required to make the seller a payment to close the equity gap.

When the seller funds the deal, a new loan is established, and it is utilized to settle any unpaid debts as well as whatever equity the seller may have in the property. Seller financing is the term for this. The borrower obtains the title to the property after the first and second mortgages are combined and "wrapped" A vendor that receives money on the first payment maintains any difference between the first and second payments. Using a wrap might help you get a mortgage at a cheaper interest rate than you otherwise would. This arrangement also benefits the seller, who is aware of your unpaid mortgage. Even if you default on your commitments, he keeps paying, and he has the authority to foreclose on your home.

Mortgage hypothecation.

You may be able to exchange the sale of an investment property for a second mortgage on your primary residence or another piece of real estate if you have a significant amount of equity in it.

A useful source of funding is a portfolio lender. By utilizing this term, banks avoid selling their own loans on the secondary market and instead hold them on hand. If you can convince them that you are an honest borrower, they could be more willing to give you money. These financial institutions include just a few others, such as Washington Mutual and World Savings. The biggest lender in the nation, Washington Mutual, has launched a mortgage financing program for first-time homebuyers that only demands a 1% down payment. When it comes to mixed-use construction finance, the great majority of portfolio lenders are quite selective about who they lend to (such as condos upstairs with retail stores below). You will want the aid of a reputable local mortgage broker that collaborates with several organizations to determine which lenders in your region are portfolio lenders and which are not. They'll be aware of who to avoid and who excels at investment loans so they can avoid them.

Finding out that a bank like Wells Fargo, which I feel is not a portfolio lender, is willing to go above and above for some of my loan applications, has been very encouraging.

Owner-financing is a fantastic method to enter the real estate market while still giving a cheap interest rate since it is free of points, fees, and other expenditures.

It is possible, but keep in mind that this is an extremely expensive and risky form of payment. Make sure you've tried everything else first, of course.

When considering borrowing money, credit cards and financial organizations should be the last two things on your mind. Finance organizations have a tough time maintaining profitability over the life of their company operations because of the very high interest rates they charge.

For renovators who aren't afraid to get their hands dirty, FHA 303(k) loans are a terrific option. The loans are returned in two installments over the course of a year. One half is handed to the seller when repairs are made, while the other half is kept in escrow until a subsequent sale of the property. If you are a recovering alcoholic or drug addict, you should consider enrolling in this program.

Your life insurance policy could have a monetary value. If you've had a life insurance policy for at least six years and are buying a property, you may be able to borrow the whole amount from it. To learn more about the requirements and repayment conditions, as well as to determine your eligibility, speak with your insurance agent.

Depending on how much money you have invested in these products, you may be able to borrow money based on the value of your mutual fund, stock, or bond holdings. If you don't pay the requisite amount, the investor has the right to seize possession of the shares.

In order to boost your retirement savings or your emergency fund, you may be qualified for a second mortgage, often known as a home equity loan, if you own your house.

Utilizing the money from your personal mortgages, you may make a down payment on a new house.
If the plan is appropriate, a self-directed IRA or qualified retirement plan may be used to complete a real estate purchase.

Loans.

The following financial choices are available to you if a flexible loan is what you need: Convertible loans (such as changing from an adjustable-rate loan to a fixed-rate loan), fixer-upper loans, and loans for borrowers who have filed for bankruptcy should all be taken into consideration while looking for a flexible lending institution.

The loan covers the whole sum.

Another party uses a certificate of deposit (CD) as a form of deposit, and the bank holds the CD in trust on behalf of all parties. Payments for interest are made to the bank. If either partner doesn't follow through on their obligations, the bank has the power to withdraw money from the CD and deposit it in another account.

Loans with less documentation requirements.

When buying a house, a significant number of self-employed people choose for loans with less paperwork. If a higher down payment is made—anywhere between 25 and 30 percent of the loan amount is acceptable—the borrower's assets and employment are only briefly discussed.
Individual investor loans could need a smaller down payment.
With as little as a 10% down payment, you may be able to get an investment loan on the open market today. Lenders could need a larger down payment since the borrower does not own the property. A flexible lender is one who is open to deviating from the standard loan practices. You would almost certainly have to pay a fee to get this kind of loan.

Individuals from other nations

Lenders with a portfolio may provide adjustable-rate loans to foreign nationals with green cards who can afford a significant down payment on their loans.

Effective and Professional Management of Institutional Lenders

Make an effort to establish permanent relationships with at least two regional lenders who specialize in real estate finance. Invite them to lunch with you. Display the whole business strategy to them. Inform them of your objectives and the outcomes you want to attain. Give them a chance to discover more about you.
Remember that the goal of all financial institutions, including banks, credit unions, and mutual funds, is to provide their customers risk-free loans. The more proof you can provide, the more likely you are to persuade them that giving you money is a prudent financial move on their behalf.
Please do not misrepresent any information to the lender. You must notify them as soon as you can if you want to purchase a rental property as an investment. You'll be shocked at how little a percentage point separates a loan for an investor from one for a borrower's primary residence. All loans issued by establishment lenders are guaranteed by the federal government. If you have an owner-occupied loan on a rental property and are found, you will likely have to answer to both the lender and the Treasury Department.

Specify any extra costs or points. As a consequence, lenders will be able to raise their profit margins.

If you plan to sell the home you purchase, a bridge loan or short-term (less than six months) private financing may be acceptable. This will give you adequate time to complete the house sale. If you don't sell your home within six months, the bank will convert your loan to a fixed-rate loan. A fixed-rate loan will almost certainly have a higher interest rate. Consider the chance that something may occur. Commercial lenders may provide qualified borrowers this kind of loan.

If you have a solid employment as a secondary source of income, it will be simpler for you to fulfill the loan's qualifying conditions. Lenders like borrowers who can utilize a variety of income sources to repay loans, and having a job makes you more appealing to lenders.

Even if you are self-employed, having the underwriters two addresses and two phone numbers on your loan application helps it seem more professional and encourages them to take it seriously.

Check to determine if there are any prepayment penalties associated with the loan you are considering. There shouldn't be any fees or penalties if you can pay back the loan with the funds you have on hand right now.

The Land Contract, the Deed Agreement, and the Deed Contract

Essentially, this is a two-party private installment purchase arrangement that was pre-arranged. The seller is protected since the deed is not transferred until the whole amount has been paid. It has sometimes been utilized to get around the due-on-sale provision. In the event of a con artist, it's feasible that the seller will be able to resell the property after receiving money. The buyer would have little chance attempting to collect on the note since it was not registered. The lender may go ahead and enforce the due on sale provision after finding that a transaction has occurred. Since the seller does not want the transaction to be documented, title insurance is not an option; only a title opinion is.

Foundations and pension funds are managed by private individuals.

A trustee, who may be a director of the foundation or an employee of the company, is normally in charge of the administration and implementation of the plan. Many individuals borrow money from other people's pension plans and charity organizations, which they later repay.

Changing the mortgage's conditions.

Many individuals are interested in mortgages, particularly seniors and those on fixed incomes. They like having the choice to make monthly contributions to bolster their income. Before you sell your house and pay off a loan for which you have been making regular payments, you should inquire with the seller about the possibility of transferring the mortgage to another property that you own or wish to purchase. Don't advocate raising interest rates to do this. If you have paid all of your payments on time and the sellers have benefited financially from the monthly installments, they may be open to extending this arrangement in the future.

For qualifying purchasers, long-term seller financing can be available.

If you can persuade the lender that you are a good credit risk, a large portion of property owners would be ready to finance the purchase of their property. After all, what could go wrong if an unknowing buyer unexpectedly stops making payments on a freshly purchased house?

In the worst-case scenario, the seller could be forced to foreclose on the property and recoup its value. Remember that they received a down payment along with a series of monthly payments (if you set up the loan that way) and that the property's worth has probably increased since you bought it.

Homeowners who understand that, unless they urgently need cash, this is not a horrible deal—especially those with significant equity or free and clear title to their property—can use this strategy. But you need money now," the store owner replies. The vast majority of sellers seek for a reasonable interest rate in order to make money from the money they get from their clients. Negotiation may be used to come to an agreement on interest rates. It depends on the nature of the commercial deal. What if you could take out a 30-year loan to pay for a home with an interest rate that was 1% higher than it was at the time? Do you think it makes sense to do that?

Regardless of whether the transaction was owner-financed or not, every deal I've worked on has resulted in a fair and amicable financing arrangement for all parties. No matter how the economy is doing, seller financing could be beneficial. The usage of seller financing may theoretically grow during times of economic trouble or when mortgage interest rates rise, among other causes. As a result, whenever you make an offer, be essential to inquire about the seller's willingness to provide financing and the terms of that agreement.

Subordination.

The seller is also aware that the buyer's other loans will take priority over the seller's lien. Consider the following illustration: An owner offers to sell you a lot for $100,000 with a $90,000 mortgage and a $10,000 down payment in return for a down payment of $10,000. Finding a regular lender that would provide a $200,000 construction loan would be challenging. You would want two-thirds of the whole loan amount since the lender sees the land as being free and clear. Your lender may use a $200,000 loan to seize both your building and your land as security for the first $600,000 mortgage. Despite the fact that you haven't paid for the lot, you've taken advantage of the equity in the seller's home to use it as collateral for your loan.

This transaction requires no upfront payment.

Deals with no down payment could be successful if the conditions are right. Negotiating with a seller to buy a property with no money down and monthly payments is not always simple. The seller must be really motivated in order to close this sale. When a home is in bad condition, it is advantageous for sellers to arrange no-money-down transactions since they know the buyer would pay for any necessary upgrades. No-down-payment acquisitions are riskier now than they were before. As real estate values rise year after year, investors may engage in highly leveraged ventures and yet come out relatively unscathed. The identical transaction is unlikely to be effective in either a stable or slow-growing economy, depending on the specifics. I would suggest staying away from no-money-down contracts based on prior experiences and the state of the economy right now. Since you have no equity, the seller is taking a tremendous risk by selling to you.

Conclusion

A building's owner who uses it as a residence or a tool for production may benefit from a stream of services given by the asset's self-consumption; a building owner who buys it as an investment may ensure a stream of future revenue.

The reasons for and significance of the factors that influence the acquisition of commodities depend on the traits and aptitudes of the operator who expresses a desire for real estate. Economic factors such as income, loan interest rates, and the level of taxes on the sale and retention of property all have an impact on consumer behavior. The demand for self-use real estate, however, may also be influenced by non-economic variables including social, psychological, and technical aspects.

On the other hand, the investor is just interested in generating money. Depending on the amount of funding available, there are different percentages of urban real estate demand that achieve these objectives. However, this percentage is especially vulnerable to changes in real estate prices and, more importantly, the performance of alternative local investments.

I hope this book has given you all the information you need to make a successful real estate investment. You should now have a good understanding of the subject. Now is the time to put all you've learned so far to work. If you exercise excellent judgment, you could become quite rich.

Ingram Content Group UK Ltd.
Milton Keynes UK
UKHW031840140323
418553UK00009B/671